The World Economy
Since The Wars

The
World Economy
Since The Wars

A PERSONAL VIEW

John Kenneth Galbraith

SINCLAIR-STEVENSON

First published in Great Britain in 1994
by Sinclair-Stevenson
an imprint of Reed Consumer Books Ltd
Michelin House, 81 Fulham Road, London SW3 6RB
and Auckland, Melbourne, Singapore and Toronto

First published in the United States in 1994
by Houghton Mifflin Company

A CIP catalogue record for this book
is available at the British Library
ISBN 1 85619 415 9

Typeset by CentraCet Limited, Cambridge
Printed and bound in Great Britain
by Mackays of Chatham plc, Chatham, Kent

For Catherine Galbraith Denholm
with love as ever

My Thanks

Those who publish books on their experience in public life have often a rather delicate task to perform. That is to offer their thanks in a suitably subtle way to the individual who actually wrote the book, while somehow minimizing this considerable delegation. Happily, I am free from such an obligation; somewhat exceptionally, I do the writing. However, my need to acknowledge my debts is not any the less.

Over the years the matters here described have been extensively discussed with Harvard and Washington colleagues and other friends over the United States and in Britain, Japan and variously in Europe. What is here pictured as my own thinking is to a marked degree what has been developed in thought and refreshed in memory by many, many others.

More specifically, I have had the help in these last months and years of my son Professor James Galbraith of the University of Texas and of his superior data banks and computer skills. To Jamie my great thanks.

My thanks also to Edith Tucker, who, as so often before, has closed up the more than occasional gaps between my recollection and historical accuracy. And to Joy Sobeck, who helped decipher my script and, more importantly, handled and frequently resisted the competing claims on my time.

But, most of all, there is my debt to Andrea Williams. For three decades and more, she has been my indispensable friend and ally. No writer ever had a more intelligent, diligent, informed and unrelenting editor. I shudder to think what would have escaped into print had she not been here.

As so often and so reliably over the last forty-two years, since I first came under their management as an author, my thanks go also to Houghton Mifflin and therein to Nader Darehshori, Joe Kanon and Mindy Keskinen, who, of all publishers, must be the most forgiving, tolerant and understanding of their authors and certainly of me.

While working on this book, I have had as always the unvarying support of Catherine Atwater Galbraith. When I turn to my writing, it is of her I think. From that come the commitment and the diligence which all authors must have. To Kitty my thanks and, most of all, my enduring love.

Contents

Contents

Introduction

As this book appears, it is sixty-one years since I began teaching economics. During this time, nearly two-thirds of the twentieth century, I have also been a more than occasional participant in economic policymaking, a fairly frequent commentator on and interpreter of economic life and, over all this time, an actively concerned observer. From that background comes this book.

It is not a history in the usual sense of the subject; I do not seek to tell all of what happened in all the interrelationship of ideas and events. That is a manifestly worthy and useful effort, but it is not mine here. This is an account of what I saw or learned of the central core of economic life in these years. I start with matters of which I heard much in my early youth, notably the grotesque tragedy of World War I, properly called the Great War, to which I later devoted attention and study. I also draw in the early chapters on other past study and writing. Thus, I was in college at the time of the great stock market speculation of the 1920s. It was not a large event in my life; it was certainly small as compared with the urgent experience of the depression that followed. But in later years I went back to examine this classic exercise in financial excess and insanity. I make use here of the resulting work, specifically my history *The Great Crash, 1929*, which was first published in 1955 and which has been in print ever since. (At any moment when it might otherwise be dropping out of sight, some new euphoric episode and the aftermath have restored it to relevance.)

But, most of all, I have relied on experience, observation and reflection. And on a reasonably capacious memory. There is, one should not doubt, an inevitable tendency to adjust interpretation to later wisdom or experience. This, as should all memoirists, I freely admit.

On some matters over the years, in such books as *The Affluent Society*, *The New Industrial State* and *Economics and the Public Purpose*, I have sought, however marginally, to influence the contemporary view of the economic and social scene. I do not here return to that effort; once is enough, and some will still think more than that. My contribution, such as it was, to the larger current of economic and social thought I leave to more detached, possibly less tolerant observers.

This, to repeat, is a book on what I saw or learned. It is not, I hasten to say or at least urge, quite all of that. I am concerned here with the main elements of economic behavior; there are many lesser matters on which I do not dwell. This is intentional. Many years ago I worked as a writer and editor under Henry Robinson Luce, founder of *Time, Fortune* and *Life* (now lost to the mergers-and-acquisitions deviance) and one of the great journalists and editors of all time. When I write, his voice still comes over my shoulder, his soft black pencil still comes down to the copy with the words 'This can go.' Detail can disguise the hard and essential core. It can also discourage as well as distract the reader. I have sought to offer here a deliberately lean account of the economic and social currents as I observed them or came to see them. Where there is more, it is less the product of intention than of personal indulgence.

In a book to come, the working title of which will be *The Lighter Side of Life*, I intend to tell of the amusements, mental aberrations and accomplished insanities that have marked and lightened life over the years. I have not entirely excluded them in the present book; prestigious stupidity, as I show in an early chapter, can be a controlling fact in economic life. In general, however, I have kept to the basic theme, which is how the economy in its larger manifestation has worked over the decades and how the influences of war and peace, government and the market, ideology and ignorance have shaped its course.

I have here, as in other writing, sought to avoid language and explanation peculiar to professional economic discourse. I do not deplore resort to this usage, sometimes called jargon; even professors of English have their professional dialect. But it has long been my view, often stated, that there is no economic process or problem that cannot be put in clear language – cannot be made accessible to the literate and interested reader. Such effect does not, however, justify error or oversimplification. In writing for the general reader one cannot claim exception from accuracy of argument or conclusion.

I delay my larger account to tell in the first chapter of my view of capitalism, the mixed economy, as an economic system – now, in the 1990s, in one form or another, the only system – and specifically of the controlling forces of change. It is my introductory and, I trust, guiding confession that I believe the greatest error in economics is in seeing the economy as a stable, immutable structure.

1

The Larger Dynamic

What is now called capitalism, or perhaps more precisely industrial capitalism, emerged in the late eighteenth century in a world dominated for hundreds of years by feudal agriculture and, in matters of economic policy, by the merchants — those who procured and sold simple, basic products, of which textiles, apparel and perhaps spices were the most obvious examples.

Although the subject is still debated, the economic system that thereafter appeared was, in substantial measure, the offspring of technology. Here the forces of change. New production methods invaded especially the textile industry. This industry was exceedingly important, for, after food and shelter, clothing is what people in both cold and temperate climates most need. To a marked extent, attire remains to this day, rather more than learning or intelligence, a prime badge of social position and distinction.

Supporting the mechanization of textile production were the water power and then the steam that drove the shuttles and looms and the steel mills that supplied the decisively important raw material for the machinery. Other supporting manufacture became necessary, as did rail and water trans-portation. And new kinds of industry developed.

The striking and accepted feature of the capitalist system was the authority with which it endowed those who owned the plant and machinery or who had the means to acquire them. The feudal and still very influential landlord owed his authority to his ownership of the land. And the merchants, including the participants in the great trading companies of earlier date – those in distant commerce to the Indies, China and the Americas – owed their importance to the ships and the money they supplied. Nonetheless, there was something seemingly distinctive about the new industrial capitalists. As compared with the ancient landed classes or the merchants, they were parvenus – new to the scene, economically com-mitted, socially crude. There was question as to how such individuals could have earned their place. More than is commonly imagined, their poor social reputation can be attributed to the adverse attitudes of the traditionally rich and favored.

Also, there was something peculiarly obvious and obtrusive about the masses of workers the plant owners mobilized and so visibly controlled. The great landlord, in descent from feudalism, had as much authority over his more widely distributed peasants as had the greatest industrialist over his assembled proletarians; it was only that the authority was less visibly exercised. From those who toiled in the fields, it exacted a traditional, rather than an overt, pecuniary response.

The industrial capitalism that developed in England and southern Scotland in the eighteenth century had the locational dynamism that survives to this day. From Britain the new system went, over the course of the next hundred years, to the German states, to France, in a more limited fashion to Scandinavia and Italy and across the Atlantic to the United States. The new American robber barons, as, amiably, they were denoted, were based primarily in New York City and were not seriously in competition with a landed aristocracy. In the 1880s and 1890s, they were the most striking manifestation of capitalist authority.

The movement continued. By the beginning of the present century there were nibblings by the new system in Russia, the most resistant of all the feudal powers. And capitalism was making its appearance, also in competition with feudal power, in Japan. In our own day it has continued on to South Korea, Taiwan, Hong Kong, Singapore, Thailand, Malaysia, mainland China and, plausibly, to India.

Just as with the beginnings of the new system in Britain, part of this development came from the simple, straightforward fact that goods and highly organized services such as transportation, communications and electricity can be supplied in far greater abundance at far lower cost and with ultimate economy of human effort by capitalist organization. Part, however, comes out of the basic dynamics of industrial production.

At the outset, there was advantage for the older, more experienced, better organized, better capitalized industry. In the last century Germany and later the United States sought protection from the more efficiently produced goods of Great Britain. (This was the infant-industries case for tariffs; the vulnerable young industry needed defense against the established and experienced older one.) But in the great dynamic of capitalism, the marked advantage of the young soon became strikingly evident. The management of industrial enterprises in the older countries became, always with exceptions, complacent and bureaucratic; that of the younger countries was eager, energetic and lean, a superiority the older countries were, not surprisingly, reluctant to concede.

More important, there was and is the matter of the labor supply. To the factories and other enterprises of the new countries streamed workers who hoped to escape the worse deprivations of feudal and peasant agriculture. For them the modest, even meager, living standards of the urban worker, as well as the new social ambience of the city, were quite wonderful as compared with the rural privation and oppression and the social isolation from which they had come. (Little in everyday attitudes is so exaggerated as the beneficence of fresh country air.) In the great dynamic of capitalism, basic industry moves relentlessly to the new, eager and economical labor force and, as will be later noticed, is retained in the older country only when that labor force is internally reinforced, as by the poor mountain whites and southern blacks in the United States or, especially in Europe, by workers recruited from foreign lands.

The advantage of the new country as to working force remains, and, in the older industrial countries, economic attitudes as ever accommodate. From the earlier demand for the protection of infant industries there comes a new demand by the older countries for the protection of aging and senile industries against the low-wage newcomers.

There is a further and relentless dynamic of capitalism. That is in its relationship to the state. This, in turn, accounts for by far the largest part of the discussion, debate and stark controversy the system provokes.

In the feudal system the great feudatories were, in fact, the government. Kings and the baronage had ample dispute, both real and recreational, one with another, but they did not question their own political eminence. That was taken for granted. In general, the merchants who gained power and authority under and after the feudal rule used the state as the instrument of their own purposes. There were grants of monopoly. Competition, in large measure from international trade, was regulated. This the new capitalists did not need or want, and it was this regulatory apparatus, known to social historians as mercantilism, that Adam Smith, the voice of the new industrialism, so vigorously and effectively attacked. Thenceforward there would be a conviction, especially in the English-speaking countries, that the state and industry were inherently at odds.

There are differences here. In Japan and Germany, two of the most successful of the capitalist states in modern times, the government and its bureaucracy are thought to be in benign, even vital, support to private industry, to capitalism. Elsewhere, and especially in the United States and Britain, government is seen, in principle and, with many exceptions, in actual practice, as the natural enemy of private enterprise. In all countries, however, the relationship of industry and the state has, over time, greatly changed, and it is central to the great dynamic of capitalism. This will be a major theme in the pages that follow.

The movement of basic or traditional industry from the older country to the new does not, of course, leave the former economically bereft; other economic activity survives and flourishes. There is continuing advantage in high and innovative technology. And after people are amply supplied with the physical objects of consumption, they move on to visual enjoyments and to entertainment. The reality is, however, that the latter – better design, better architecture, theatrical and television productions, fashion, art, intellectual pursuits – do not have the same aspect of economic substance as do steel mills or automobile factories. This is a fact based not in economics but again in historic and traditional attitudes. The steel mills came first; they seem, as does their product, to be the solid basis of economic life.

Economic growth is the further dynamic of capitalism. In modern times such growth – the increase in the aggregate production of goods and services expressed in statistical terms – has become the accepted test of economic performance. An economy, like a healthy adolescent, is assumed to have an inherent commitment thereto. 'We may expect a 4.1 percent rate of growth in the next quarter.' No other statistic in modern times has a more compelling authority. For economists and many others, the rate of growth is *the* dynamic of modern capitalism.

Economic growth and its extraordinary social and political effects are important in what follows. Important also is its extreme unreliability. This has two aspects.

There is, first, the tendency of capitalism to grave instability. Built into the system are recurrent episodes of devastation. Growth slows, gives way to absolute decline. Confidence and comfort give way to fear and distress. This has long been so, but it has frequently not been conceded. In the last century in the United States such episodes were called 'crises' or 'panics.' These terms were soon thought to convey fear and to have an adverse effect on business morale, and there was recourse to the much milder term 'depression.' 'Not a panic, only a depression.' 'Depression' then acquired the deeply adverse connotation of the grim economic experience of the 1930s, and from the search for a less disturbing term, the word 'recession' came into use. 'It is not a depression, only a recession.' As 'recession' then established its own unpleasant meaning, there was an effort to substitute 'growth adjustment.' Whatever it is called, depression, recession, growth adjustment or, a most grievous modern thought, 'an enduring underemployment equilibrium' and the causes thereof play an important role in any view of the modern economy in its world setting.

Second, there is the large part of the planet where there is no appreciable economic growth or where deteriorating living standards are the norm. This is true of much of Africa, of Central and much of South America and of parts of Asia. In general economic discussion, this world lies apart, but if we are concerned with human values and human suffering, it must be at the center of our concern. Against the achievements of modern economic life must be set its failures. Of this, also, I seek to be conscious in the pages to come.

Traditionally the economic textbooks concluded with a chapter or chapters called 'comparative economic systems.' Attention was there turned to the planning and command system of comprehensive socialism, commonly called Communism, in which all or most productive resources are owned by the state or, in the preferred language, the people. From the state come the initiative and instruction as to what is to be produced.

Now, in these last years, as this is written, these final chapters have been rendered nugatory, without purpose or force. In the greatest economic change of modern times, perhaps of all time, socialism as an alternative system has been relegated to the distant and ambiguous world of Cuba, North Korea, and maybe still China. This change, too, must loom large in any view of the economic world in the twentieth century. So it does here.

We should not, however, be too extreme in our view. In recent years, and in consequence, in no slight measure, of the collapse of Communism just mentioned, the name of Karl Marx, which was once a symbol of fear, has now become an object of disdain. It would be unfortunate were this carried too far. In large part, we owe to Marx the concept of economic determinism, an understanding of the powerful and even decisive role of economic forces in the shaping of human history. That was true a century and a half ago when Marx's ideas and system were being formed; it is not less true today. It invites attention beyond that of professional economists, for while modern history cannot be confined within economic parameters, neither can it be understood without knowledge of the shaping and controlling economic context. Over the years, and therefore here, I have been much concerned with seeing how economics and economic change affect and dominate the larger social, political and military scene.

2

The Great Divide

I was born in Canada in 1908 and thus was six years old in 1914 when World War I broke out. I cannot lay claim to any great depth of economic perception at that time nor four years later when it ended and when, in a slightly premature way, I was entering high school. But these cruel and tremendous years remain rich in my memory; the death and sorrow reached into rural Ontario, as did, quite visibly, the opposition to the war and its slaughter. There was strong feeling, especially among the rural Scotch, as correctly we were called, that the wrong people were in charge of things and that they were congenitally stupid. These were conclusions that in later years, as I went back to read and to study about the war, I did not change. In effect, they are what I here affirm. But there was more.

I am persuaded, as indeed have been many others, that the great turning point of modern economic history, the one that more than any other ushered in the modern economic era, was the Great War of 1914–1918, since reduced to the more modest and, on the whole, less accurate and expressive designation of World War I. It shattered a political structure that had been dominant in Europe for centuries. And it greatly altered the position of the United States on the world economic scene. From being an addendum to, even an afterthought in, economic discussion, the United States became the centerpiece. The lights of London and Paris were not dimmed; it was only that those of New York came more brilliantly into view.

In a much-quoted passage, John Maynard Keynes observed that 'it is ideas, not vested interests, which are dangerous for good or evil.'[1] I share the desire of all scholars to believe that ideas are a compelling force, but I am led here to urge the rather more traumatic power of events. Besides destroying a political and economic structure that had been long in place, the war reshaped for all ensuing time the relationship between nations great and small, rich and impoverished. The change it initiated was not clear or decisive; years of incoherence, both economic and political, followed. Yet there should be no doubt that the change was monumental. The First World War was, indeed, rightly called the Great War; World War II was its last battle.

What came to an end in Europe was a political and economic system, one easily visible in Germany, Eastern Europe and Imperial Russia, less evident in Britain and, as ever, more ambiguous in France. For centuries political authority in Europe had been, to a greater or lesser degree, associated

---

1. John Maynard Keynes, *The General Theory of Employment Interest and Money* (New York: Harcourt, Brace, 1936), p. 384. In the original title there were no commas, but commentators or their well-meaning editors have invariably added them.

---

with landed proprietorship or, at a minimum, with a landed aristocratic tradition. So also, and more markedly, had military power. Beneath this ruling caste came the ancient merchant class and the capitalists, who, as noted, had replaced the artisans of an earlier time with the mass production and distribution of goods and the provision of transportation services.

Government, nonetheless, was still considered the responsibility of the old landed or onetime feudal classes. For centuries social position and political prestige were accorded to the ownership of land or a privileged access to its revenues. Those who ruled, to repeat, were the surviving expression of this landed power, as especially was the officer class in the armies. In Britain, along with France the most conspicuously democratic of the major European powers, it was still a serious social and political disqualification to be 'in trade.' Businessmen, financiers, went their own way. It was not the natural function of those so engaged to govern, to be in Parliament or certainly to serve as officers in the armed forces. In much writing and discussion, an image of power was attributed to the leading capitalists – those who owned or financed the industrial establishments and, to a large extent, the railroads – but this in no way reflected the reality in Europe. It reflected, instead, the persuasive voice of Karl Marx. Marx, like Adam Smith and more than any other figure in economics except perhaps Keynes, has the distinction of greatly influencing the thought of the many who have never read him.

Even among the strongly established Liberals in Britain there was still reference and deference to the landed ruling class. It was only four years before the war that the powers of the House of Lords and its hereditary caste had been effectively curbed. In the British Army the ruling class and the officer class were largely identical.

In Berlin and even more noticeably in Vienna and St. Petersburg, the ancient power of the landed aristocrats remained fully dominant in the government and the military establishment. They, not the bourgeoisie or the industrialists, made the decisions to go to war and to prepare, especially in the case of Germany, the meticulous plans for conducting it. In Germany, again under the influence of Marx, there was an admitted tendency to look beyond the ancient ruling class to the modern industrial power of Krupp, but the reality of power was still with the landed elite.

There were notable consequences of this continuing role of the old feudal classes. One was the profound centuries-old instinct that war has primarily to do with landed territory. Once, indeed, this had been true: territorial conquest *was* traditionally the basis of both wealth and power. With land came economically productive peasants, public and personal revenues and men available to wage armed combat for their master. Accordingly, wars were fought for the highly practical purpose of winning more territory. This being so, defensive military thought turned to frontiers; these must be manned and fortified. The possession of Alsace and Lorraine was central to relations between France and Germany. The possession of Poland was a decisive issue farther to the east. The lust to possess land (as well as also, to be sure, to acquire and preserve trading privileges) reached out to Africa, Asia and the Middle East. Few ideas have lodged so deeply in the human psyche while occasioning so little comment. There were continuing powerful echoes of this ancient attitude during World War II in Adolf Hitler's demand for *Lebensraum* and in the territorial adjustments and acquisitions in Eastern Europe and the Baltic states after the war was over. The feudal notion that war has to do with the defense of landed territory, the safeguarding of vulnerable frontiers, still lurks today in the deeper recesses of the military mind, or what is commonly so denoted.

It was to be one of the modern and more welcome triumphs of capitalist attitude and achievement to diminish this acquisitive need for more land. In the highly prosperous city-states of Singapore and Hong Kong, land has been shown to be wholly irrelevant. And in the larger world it came eventually to be realized that colonial territory was only marginally relevant to economic progress, if it was relevant at all. In the years after the Second War, Britain, France, Belgium and the Netherlands, as well as the United States, all shed their colonial possessions; scarcely a ripple was felt in their domestic economic well-being. The dissidence and revolt of the colonial peoples and a more civilized attitude by the colonial powers are often credited with bringing the colonial era to an end. More attention might well be accorded to the rather simple but persuasive fact that colonies had become no longer economically worthwhile. Territory was no longer the thing. Of this, more later.

Associated with the possession of ancestral land and the accompanying tradition was the vital matter of human intelligence. Inheritance was by right, not by mental ability or qualification.

*

Growing up in rural Canada amidst the Scottish clans of the region, I heard much, as I have said, of the manifest stupidity of the conflict in Europe, of any Canadian participation, and of the leaders, military and civilian, so involved. Intelligent men, it was believed, did not lend themselves to such insanity. There was even local confirmation. One evening I went with my parents to a community meeting in the nearby village hall. Two uniformed recruiting officers – it was before conscription – used the occasion to make speeches designed to persuade the young farmers and farm hands in the assembly to enlist. Asked who would operate the farms in their absence, one officer replied with vehemence, 'What does it matter if this country grows up in weeds from the Atlantic to the Pacific so long as we save it?' The need for food had not occurred to him. For me, no doubt by way of my father, this interchange provided compelling support to the larger local belief in the ignorance of those running the war.

Ignorance, stupidity, in great affairs of state is not something that is commonly cited. A certain political and historical correctness requires us to assign some measure of purpose, of rationality, even where, all too obviously, it does not exist. Nonetheless one cannot look with detachment on the Great War (and also its aftermath) without thought as to the mental insularity and defectiveness of those involved and responsible. The aristocratic and landed tradition was, indeed, a nearly perfect design for ensuring that both government and the armed forces would be in the hands of leaders of minimal competence. Selection was by inheritance, not by intelligence. As noted, even the intellectually most impaired individuals, if otherwise qualified by birth and bearing, could ascend to major positions of civil and military power. And they did.

Russia was, without doubt, the extreme case. The late Barbara Tuchman, in her classic account of the background and early days of the war, says of Czar Nicholas II, 'he ruled as an autocrat and was in turn ruled by his strong-willed if weak-witted wife.'[2] The German Kaiser Wilhelm, who was himself endowed with a limited personal intelligence, thought the Czar ' "only fit to live in a country house and grow turnips." '[3] The Imperial Russian Minister of War, Vladimir Sukhomlinov, was indolent, unintelligent and known to conserve his energy more or less exclusively for the sexual demands of his very young wife. He took a strong stand against all military innovation more recent than the cavalry charge. In this and other views and actions involving the army he was strongly supported by the Czar.

The Austro-Hungarian Empire, an incoherent assemblage of ethnic, religious and language groupings created by territorial acquisition, had long been verging on dissolution. Under the aged leadership of Franz Josef – he was now in his mid-eighties – it was, with Russia, the most fragile manifestation of the old order. Vienna, a center, like Paris, renowned for the sophistication of its cultural and intellectual life, did not extend this distinction either to the armed forces or to the state. In those areas, again by inheritance, the near monopoly of the ignorant prevailed. That the leadership and military command of so fragile a structure should have risked a major war will long stand as a marvel of mental vacuity.

2. Barbara W. Tuchman, *The Guns of August* (New York: Macmillan, 1962), p. 8.
3. Ibid.

In the other warring countries, not excluding Britain and France, political and military leadership also descended to minimal levels of intellectual competence. Britain's Prime Minister H. H. Asquith, who was socially reputable, eventually became too visibly inadequate and was replaced in the middle of the conflict by the markedly more able (and more proletarian) David Lloyd George. The Admiralty and a major role in strategic planning were accorded by right of birth to the young Winston Churchill, a scion of Britain's greatest house. His unquestioned intelligence was not matched at that time by experience or judgment, and, as a major consequence, he was the architect of the Dardanelles campaign, the most luminous catastrophe of the war, although there can be little doubt that responsibility for it was shared with remarkably incompetent generals and admirals. In Churchill's case, maturity and experience brought eventual and brilliant redemption, but not before a further and grave economic aberration, which will presently be mentioned. Field Marshal Horatio Herbert Kitchener, the Secretary for War, sailed to Russia on a secret mission aboard the ill-fated cruiser *Hampshire* in June 1916. Whitehall's regret over the loss of the ship at sea was considerably tempered by the simultaneous loss of Kitchener. Sir John French, the first commander of the British forces in France, is, indeed, greatly celebrated by the historians of the period for his committed inadequacy. So is Sir Douglas Haig, one of the mentally more immobile military figures of that age. He returned to Britain after the war to a richly deserved anonymity, from which he once emerged to assert that the next war would be won by a decisive cavalry charge.

In Germany Field Marshal Paul von Beneckendorff und

von Hindenburg and in France Marshal Henri Philippe Pétain, who were both enhanced by the glow of presumed military achievement, were later tested in civilian political positions. For both, and for their countries, it was an unmitigated disaster.

The controlling role of tradition in the warring nations was also strongly reflected in the conduct of the war. Naval warfare, which was somewhat outside the province of the traditional military class, *was* technologically quite advanced. Ships could destroy each other with remarkable effectiveness at a distance of several miles, and submarines were a major and damaging innovation. On land, however, tradition ruled. Observation aircraft, heavier guns, poison gas, all made an appearance, as belatedly did tanks. But mostly men assailed each other with rifles and bayonets as they had for generations, with only the machine gun, often badly deployed, making the passage more perilous than before. Along with the men, an impressive number of horses were used on or near the battlefields in France, and, not surprisingly, they proved vulnerable to even a single old-fashioned bullet.

The views of those in the old political and economic structure were manifested most remarkably, however, in the attitude toward the common soldiers. Extensively the latter were still recruited from the land. Since ancient times, they had been generally associated in the minds of the landlords with the livestock; they were, like the cattle, a disposable resource. In Germany, France and Britain, there was more than a passing question prior to the war as to how the massed urban proletariat would respond, and conscription was long delayed in Britain partly for that reason. As to the peasantry, however, there were few doubts; they were dispersed over the land and fully under control. And by the old aristocracy who were in charge, their slaughter was viewed numerically – how many casualties by routine military calculation could or could not be afforded or, as was commonly said, accepted. The contained agony of the common soldier facing more or less certain death did not qualify for serious thought.

This view was generally held in Europe, and the statistics affirm the point. Figures assembled in 1924 by the United States War Department, as it then was, put the total of mobilized forces from all countries at 65 million. Of these, 8.5 million were killed or died, 21.2 million were wounded, and another 7.7 million were taken prisoner or were missing. For those in uniform during the war, the chance of undamaged survival was well under 50 percent. Here clearly the human cost of ignorance.

That the landed territory of the United States did not suffer any physical damage in the First World War, as again in World War II, has been often remarked. Also the American participation in the First War – a year and a half – was relatively brief. But most important, the United States, in lesser measure even than France and Britain and in marked contrast with Germany, Austria-Hungary, the other Eastern European countries and Imperial Russia, did not have an economic and associated political system that was at risk. Land ownership was widely distributed in the North and West; there was no recognizable landed or landlord class. There was no readily identifiable military tradition. To the extent that there was a privileged aristocracy, it comprised the great capitalists, not any ancient or established ruling class. The responsibility for the war was delegated to professionals, and, on the whole, it would appear they handled it with competence.

The United States was not, however, altogether without proof of the defective role of a ruling feudal aristocracy. This was sadly, even disastrously, evident in the states of the old Confederacy. Slavery, the most ostentatious manifestation of feudal power, had been eliminated a half century earlier, but the successor plantation system, with the erstwhile slaves now become sharecroppers, had, in highly significant measure, survived. The former slaves and their black or hybrid descendants did not vote or otherwise participate in any way in their government. Writing of the slave economy, Eugene D. Genovese, a noted authority, cited its 'retardative effects.' 'A low level of capital accumulation, the planters' high propensity to consume luxuries, a shortage of liquid capital aggravated by the steady drain of funds out of the region, the low productivity of slave labor . . . the anti-industrial, anti-urban ideology of the dominant planters,' along with the minimal purchasing power of the slaves, all assured a primitive and stagnant economy.[4] Had the whole economy and polity of the United States been that of the American South, the country would not have played a decisive role in World War I or, for that matter, in either of the two wars. Here, too, was an indication of the economically incompetent role of feudal landed power.

A half century earlier – in the South, too, it might be noted

4. Eugene D. Genovese, 'The Significance of the Slave Plantation for Southern Economic Development,' in *The Political Economy of Slavery: Studies in the Economy and Society of the Slave South* (New York: Pantheon Books, 1965), p. 158.

– there had also been irresponsibly precipitated conflict. Firing on Fort Sumter and inviting war with the industrially far more advanced and powerful North was remarkably similar to Germany's reckless proclamation of unrestricted submarine warfare on January 31, 1917, and the attack on Pearl Harbor by a highly traditionalist Japan on December 7, 1941.

On the whole, industrial democracy served the United States, if not perfectly, at least better than it did the feudal residue in Europe. American soldiers met the enemy only in the last months of the war. The total of their dead, if far from minimal – 116,000[5] – was small compared with the 1,350,000 Frenchmen, 950,000 from the British Empire, perhaps 1,600,000 Germans, 1,450,000 from Austria-Hungary and a wildly estimated 2,300,000 Russians.[6] However, the American industrial commitment was not great or decisive. The constraints of time meant that the industrial mobilization in the United States was far from effective. No Germans were killed by American artillery, some armament on ships apart. Lloyd George marveled in his memoirs that a country industrially so significant could have contributed so little in usable weaponry and other physical instruments of war. Other writers have thought him less than generous, but the point need not be pursued here. The United States had a marginal role in this disaster; what is important is what this war (as

5. According to the Veterans Administration Office of Public and Consumer Affairs.
6. Marc Ferro, *The Great War, 1914–1918* (London: Routledge and Kegan Paul, 1973), Table 4, p. 227.

also World War II) did for the world position of the Great Republic. To a marked degree, modern American economic achievement is built on the errors of the European (and later the Japanese) ruling classes.

I now turn to the distinctly elementary economics of the war and of wartime finance and the deeply incoherent aftermath as I came to see them over the years.

3

The Roots of Disorder

In 1941, as I will later tell, I was placed in charge of price control (and for a time also of rationing) in the emerging defense program and, after Pearl Harbor, in the Second World War. Mine was by any calculation one of the three or four, maybe half-dozen, critical posts in the management of the wartime economy and was part of a larger task for which there was more than ample precedent. A mere twenty-three years earlier, economic policy or its absence had been central in the conduct of the Great War. I became immersed in that earlier experience in joint study with others, through reading and principally through the firsthand advice and guidance of some of those who had participated, especially the ever-present Bernard Baruch, who had been in charge of wartime industrial mobilization in the First War. All but exclusively, it was seen as an exercise in errors to be avoided.

Before going on to the lessons of World War I as they affected and even controlled later thought, I must point out the larger influences operating on wartime attitudes and the political and economic response thereto. It is not the professional tendency of the economist to minimize the role of economics and economic decision. However, where war is concerned, there is the larger effect of politics and anthropology.

In the years following the Great War, economic disorientation and disorder had their undoubted role. In Russia, Germany, Austria-Hungary and other of the Eastern European lands, the trauma of defeat was combined with the destruction of an old and established political structure. Open was the question as to what would take its place. And from this came the struggle, severe and sometimes violent, to fill the vacuum.

Of the obvious contenders for leadership, the politically most mature and enlightened by far were the socialists, the capitalist proletariat. And they had temporary successes in Germany, Austria and most especially in Russia. There, though limited in numbers, they were effectively led against an old order that had become a political and social void. Elsewhere the socialists lacked a workable economic design, a sufficient political base and thus the supporting economic, political (and military) power.

Socialism, the comprehensive operation or control of industry by the state, existed in superbly attractive form in oratory, in literature and in belief, but in its administrative complexity and call upon the sense of social responsibility of the citizen it was not a viable design, and certainly not in the extreme disorganization of defeat. There was, accordingly, no workable alternative to the self-motivated firm and proprietor and the market. Even in Russia, where the armies of Leon Trotsky established the requisite power base, Lenin, under the decisive force of economic circumstance, had to retreat to the market in the New Economic Policy, this to be reversed in later times by Joseph Stalin and then, with grave and contentious chaos, reversed once again in our own day.

In Britain and France there was also articulate challenge to the established order but no serious revolutionary activity. Nor was there in the United States. Capitalism, tempered by democratic process, was showing itself to be a relatively secure economic system; the vulnerability that Marx and Engels had foreseen did not materialize. The eventual threat it would face would be not from an angry, motivated proletariat but, as the later years would reveal, from its own internal tendency to inequality in economic reward and a pattern of speculative excess, followed by general economic deprivation and the inevitable political and social response.

More important as a noneconomic force in the immediate aftermath of the war, as indeed following all wars, was anthropology. This is very much a part of the historical experience, yet it is a matter that is little subject to formal analytical comment.

In the tribal community, when the drums sound in the adjacent forest, there is an automatic response. The tribesmen rally to the enthusiasm of battle and the mystic enhancement of the chieftain. Then, following either victory or defeat, there is the reaction. Reason returns. Reflection is not on what has been gained but on what has been endured. The leaders are blamed, reviled and rejected. In the modern world this sequence still remains.

Among the casualties of both modern victory and defeat are those who have led in the war. Woodrow Wilson, in declining health and prestige, had his treaty and the League of Nations decisively rejected by the Congress, as his party was rejected in 1920. Lloyd George saved himself temporarily by the election he called within days after the armistice, but, later and reluctantly, he largely passed from sight. Georges Clemenceau, who held together a dismayed and fractious country from 1917 on and who was the strongest voice for retribution therapy at the Versailles Conference – the word conference is here loosely used, for the terms of the treaty were dictated firmly, unilaterally, to the Germans – was soon retired from office. Anticipating what would soon become routine for failed statesmen, he went on a speaking tour of the United States. The leader of the Canadian forces, General Sir Arthur Currie, returned from the war to a hero's welcome, the post of principal of McGill University and a major libel suit growing out of the charge that in the last hours of the hostilities he had let his soldiers be killed unnecessarily in a final self-serving assault so that he could better position himself for the victory.

Needless to say, the opposing tribal leaders fell into even more violent disrepute. The Kaiser went into permanent exile in Holland, which resisted his extradition for war crimes. The Hapsburgs, the ancient ruling family, were banned permanently from Vienna. The Czar, having suffered earlier defeat, was summarily shot, along with his wife and children.

In the later experience of World War II, the now richly experienced Winston Churchill, the most dominant and successful of the wartime leaders, was promptly denied office once the war was over. It is at least interesting to imagine that President Roosevelt escaped this remorseless anthropology of conflict by an early, well-timed death. No one was surprised that neither Hitler and Mussolini nor the more anonymous Japanese military leaders survived defeat. Even Emperor Hirohito, though in a passive role throughout the war, was thought in the aftermath to be in a somewhat perilous position, his continued existence dependent on American support.

The common soldier suffers during the conflict, but, at the end, the anthropology of war deals most sternly with those responsible for its conduct. It is a warning to all. A closer knowledge of these adverse rites would have told Lyndon Johnson what to expect even had there been victory in Vietnam, and George Bush what would follow his seeming success in the Persian Gulf.

The anthropological reaction is powerful, but a word must now be said on the economic factors as they operated in the Great War and contributed to the ensuing disorder.

What in suitably formidable language has been called economic mobilization for war is, like so much in economics, a relatively obvious thing. It involves, by one design or another, the movement of manpower, materials, plant and its production from civilian to military use. Included is the movement of individuals, men and, in World War II especially, women without previous productive employment, into war-supporting jobs, including those vacated by the individuals mobilized into the military forces. There are essentially three ways of arranging this transfer; all were used in World War I. In all countries, including the United States, this was done with the incoherence that so comprehensively characterized this conflict. By World War II, there was a fairly rational design for economic mobilization in all countries; in the First War there was none. Economic action was strictly ad hoc; that for which the circumstance of the moment seemed to call, the politics of the time seemed to allow.

The three ways of transferring manpower and physical plant and resources into wartime use are by force, by payment for the needed transfer from funds collected by taxation and by payment from money printed or otherwise created for the purpose – in common language, by inflation.

Notable in World War I was the fiscally economical use of force. The vast armies assembled for the conflict were, in the main, drafted; that is, compelled to their task. The European combatants were paid only insignificant sums – a few pence or centimes a day. Little mention has been made in the literature of wartime finance of how effectively by this means the cost of the war was placed on those whom it also put at greatest risk. There was surprise and even some unhappiness that American, Australian and Canadian soldiers were more adequately compensated for their service, the Americans and Canadians at the seemingly extravagant level of around a dollar a day.

It is, to repeat, one of the less celebrated facts of the war that the ordinary infantrymen were expected to combine both economic and supreme sacrifice. In certain cases they did express discontent. Dissatisfaction as to leave and other amenities led to the potentially disastrous 1917 mutiny in the French Army; the better-educated, socially more conscious Russian military-school cadets and German naval enlisted men reacted adversely in Petrograd in 1917 and in Kiel in 1918. It was the news that the revolution had made land available back home as an alternative to the unpaid service they were performing that caused Russian recruits to vote with their feet and so to end their and their country's participation in the war. Nonetheless, nothing is more surprising than the relative ease with which the economic burdens of the war were imposed on the common soldier. Patriotism demanded no less. Who could challenge that?

Taxation was a far more difficult matter. Its purpose was sufficiently to restrain domestic expenditure and consumption so that manpower and materials were set free for military employment. From stern taxation, grave problems of morale were thought to arise – an overtaxed populace might lose its commitment to the war. (In World War II, there was still such fear; a proposal by Franklin Roosevelt that, for the duration, incomes be limited by taxation to $25,000 a year – now about $250,000 – was indignantly, even emotionally, rejected.)

All of the belligerents in World War I did raise taxes, on, variously, incomes, profits, excess profits, consumer goods, and in keeping with no consistent design. The United States imposed levies on toilet articles, chewing gum, telephone and telegraph communications and freight and express charges. The income tax, newly available because of the Republican initiative of President William Howard Taft, was now brought into wartime use. The basic rate was increased from what had been a flat 1 percent in 1913 to a graduated, seemingly painful 6 percent on the first $4,000 and 12 percent on incomes over that amount in 1918. Surtax rates went up from 1 percent on incomes over $20,000 and 6 percent on incomes over $500,000 in 1913 to as high as 65 percent on incomes over $1,000,000 in 1918. The corporate income tax, at 1 percent in 1913, went to 12 percent by 1918.[1] The profits of munitions makers, which were very good, attracted a

1. Catherine Ruggles Gerrish, 'Public Finance and Fiscal Policy, 1866–1918,' in *The Growth of the American Economy*, 2nd ed., edited by Harold F. Williamson (New York: Prentice Hall, 1951), p. 639.

special levy. The total American expenditure for the war is estimated to have been just under $35 billion, including loans to the Allies of around $9 billion; about a third of the direct outlay of $26 billion was covered by taxes, and the rest was covered by borrowing.[2] The European belligerents had similar, though highly diverse, divisions as between what was gathered by taxation and what was borrowed.

From the borrowing came the third means of paying for the war, and this had the most enduring effect. It was inflation – the simple intrusion of virginally created government purchasing power into the economy to serve wartime purposes. In this fashion, goods and labor were bid away from private use with the consequent effect on prices.

In the American Civil War, responding to the hard-pressed needs of the time, the Secretary of the Treasury, Salmon Portland Chase, simply ordered the printing of money, the immortal greenbacks, to pay for the support of the Union armies. By 1914, there was a more subtle design, although reference to the forthright printing of money by the government remained common, as indeed it does to this day.

The new and more refined procedure was to sell bonds to the public in the hope that the money so surrendered would take the place of private expenditure. Were increased saving so induced, room would be made for government wartime purchases without an increase in the total demand for goods and services. Such an effort was made with much patriotic fervor, persuasion and oratory. This responded to a deep conviction that in such fashion the war could be paid for

2. Ibid., p. 640.

without larger economic effect. In fact, it can be assumed that much, perhaps most, of the money used to buy the government-issued Liberty Bonds, thrift stamps and war-savings certificates would have been saved in any case. The bonds were also security for loans and resulting expenditure. So the claims on the economy were increased as the proceeds from the loans were spent. Public fraud of the more amiable type regularly captures the minds of those who perpetrate it.

More important, however, was the sale of bonds to banks and, in the case of the United States, to the newly created Federal Reserve banks. This put deposits at the command of the government, against which war payments could be made. Money, purchasing power, was as surely obtained in this fashion as by the earlier and cruder resort to Salmon Chase's printing press. That a bank balance accords the government the same right of purchase as printed money none on reflection will doubt. However, the process also involves some printing, for some part of the expanded deposits was converted to cash for hand-to-hand payment. The provision of currency for the conversion of deposits into cash as the latter was needed remained a subsidiary, even routine, function of the government. Added to this government-created purchasing power in the United States was a massive inflow of gold to pay for the purchases of the friendly European belligerents, Britain and France, which after 1917 became the Allies. The inflow was to make the United States the effective repository of the world's gold stocks in the generations to come.

The flush new purchasing power from the spending of money thus borrowed from the central bank did take men, plant, materials and weaponry into wartime use. It accomplished this by bidding up prices, denying consumption to those who had fixed incomes or who were relying on previously accumulated savings. Private consumption was pressed down effectively, even relentlessly, by the higher prices. The resulting deprivation served the war and, not slightly, those whose selling prices and incomes had been enhanced by the higher prices.

Finally, the inflation lodged in bank accounts and pockets sums of money not spent but saved for future use. Sadly, this money and its eventual expenditure could ensure that the inflation would not end with the coming of peace. It might even become worse, and so in all countries in 1919 (and, in some, later) it did.

In the United States wholesale prices had about doubled by the end of the war. The increase in France was much greater, while that in Britain and Germany was only slightly less.

In the years that followed, there would be major legacies of the war finance. One, just mentioned, was from the gold flows to the United States. These and the loans they could sustain would, as I've indicated, establish the United States in general and New York City in particular as the world financial center. Borrowers large and small, public and private, would now make their way to Wall Street. This traffic would be especially evident in the decade of the 1920s.

The method of war finance, the ease in creating purchasing power, would also have a future. In the war's immediate aftermath there would be the great inflations in Germany and Austria. What served in war would be truly exploited come the peace.

While inflation, created by the borrowing from the banks and expenditure from the accounts so created, is a compelling alternative to taxation, it is not, in the longer run, less painful. Those who see their previous savings become worthless, those who lend money only to have a diminished value returned, those who have fixed incomes, all remember the pain. So they do to this day in Germany and Austria. In the United States, as World War II approached, the fear of inflation and the need for its prevention were emphasized hardly less than the procurement of weapons. It was in the context of this fear that I took over the control of prices in 1941, my view of inflation enhanced by the earlier study I had made of the postwar financial disorder and disorientation. It is to the economically unpredictable years after World War I that I now turn attention.

4

Debt, Inflation and John Maynard Keynes

As I have said, my reading and eventual government responsibilities taught me about war mobilization and its effects in
the First War. Two books involved me in the great and
luminous events that followed. One of the first serious
volumes that I read on economics outside the current of
assigned and compelled texts was John Maynard Keynes's
The Economic Consequences of the Peace.[1] Then in later times I
was much influenced by the classic study of the great German
inflation of the early 1920s[2] and by its author, Frank D.
Graham, long the leading light of the Princeton University
Department of Economics. He was one of my closest and
most admired friends until the sad day when, subject to deep
and perhaps inadequately treated depression, he went to a
Princeton football game and, at the end, threw himself over
the encircling wall of the stadium.

*

1. New York: Harcourt, Brace and Howe, 1920.
2. Frank D. Graham, *Exchange, Prices, and Production in Hyper-Inflation: Germany,
1920–1923* (Princeton: Princeton University Press, 1930).

Few episodes in world history have been more meticulously studied than the Versailles Conference of 1919, the role of each of the several participants and the consequences, which extended on to World War II. In broad substance, however, its basic preoccupations were four: there was the powerful expression of the old concern for the possession and now the dispossession of landed area and associated ethnic communities. In consequence, Germany surrendered Alsace and Lorraine back to France, and territory was also given to Belgium and Denmark, while the new Poland was carved out in the East. The overseas territory of Germany, the German African and Pacific island colonial domain, was, of course, taken away. There was similar and intense concern for the dismemberment of the old Austro-Hungarian Empire and as to where the pieces should go. The feeling, the deeper sense, that war has to do with the possession of land was fully served.

Second, there was the determination that Germany should not reemerge as a military power. Accordingly, the German Navy was sent over to Britain (and there scuttled), future German land forces were limited as to size, and the Rhineland was forbidden to German soldiers.

The third preoccupation, the one most debated in the United States, involved the creation of an organization, the League of Nations, to oversee the peace and, it was hoped, to ensure against renewed conflict and disaster.

Fourth and finally, and of primary relevance to my generation of economists, was the matter of money.

On this the Versailles conferees and a special reparations commission established to work on amounts and details had a view that was almost grotesquely simple, as perhaps befitted those advancing it. Germany had started the war; it had

invaded Belgium, gone on into France with heavy destruction
there and involved in an exceedingly costly way the British,
the Americans and the Italians, all of whom were now at the
conference. For this, quite clearly, it should be made to pay;
the bill for the war should now be passed to the Reich. The
total was not small: the principal belligerents submitted
claims of about $40 billion, which would be the equivalent of
rather more than $400 billion in current dollars and was a
sum that bore no conceivable relation to postwar Germany's
ability to pay. The cost of repairing wartime damage – in this
case, from the devastated landscape in France to the tor-
pedoed *Lusitania* – is never slight. So the logic seemed
inescapable: the Germans started it, they did the damage,
they lost the war. Now, very simply, they were fully liable.

There was a further, more strictly economic factor to be
considered. To pay for needed materials from abroad, France
(as also Italy and Russia) had borrowed heavily from Britain,
and Britain and France, but notably Britain, had borrowed
billions – approximately $8.7 billion – from the United States.
Surely no one could doubt the justice in having the Germans
assume these debts. In later days, when they had not done
so, and when there was urgent talk in Washington of forgiving the British and French debt – the inter-Allied debt –
President Calvin Coolidge was adamant in expressing the
reputable economic mood of the time: 'They hired the
money, didn't they?'

So it was decided. The only matter that was not decided
was how Germany would pay. Some reparations could be in
kind, and France laid claim to substantial shipments of coal
from the German mines. But money, hard cash, was the
obvious answer. Unfortunately the money payments, as a

practical matter, could only be made out of a surplus in the German international accounts – an excess of revenues from exports over imports sufficient to cover an acceptable annual payment. Such a surplus, in turn, could only be arranged were the Germans to forgo dependence on imported goods and, from superior productive efficiency and lower wage costs, create a sufficient advantage for its products in foreign markets. The loss of the German market – of sales to Germany – would have to be accepted by those countries receiving the reparations and all others too.

There was another problem: the German government would have to tax or otherwise appropriate in order to recover the income from the surplus in the international accounts – the revenues accruing from exports and going to business firms and on to owners, executives and even workers. Only after the funds were so collected could they be sent abroad. All this would have to be accomplished in a country experiencing not only the trauma of defeat but also the transfer of governing power from the ancient and traditional rulers to the new, avowedly, if not actually, socialist regime, which was involved, inevitably, in a contest for supremacy with both the old ruling class and the broad capitalist interest.

Little or none of this was discussed at Versailles or afterward, certainly not in formal debate. To repeat: Germany had invaded to the West; Germany should pay. The problem of how was a detail. Insanity based on seeming logic was the order of the day.

So the economic problem would have remained, awaiting hard experience and then the historians, except for a young member of the British peace delegation in Paris: John Maynard Keynes. From Keynes now came the first of the two most influential tracts on economics in the first half of the twentieth century: his attack on the Versailles Treaty, the already mentioned *Economic Consequences of the Peace*. The second book of significance was also by Keynes, and about it there will be more to come.

John Maynard Keynes, thirty-one at the beginning of the war, educated at Eton and Cambridge, briefly a civil servant, then a Cambridge don, was already marked as a young man of diverse interests and effective thought. (Doing badly on economic questions on his civil service examinations, he had observed, no doubt correctly, that his examiners obviously knew less of the subject than did he.) He spent the war in the British Treasury handling the varied problems having to do with conserving and allocating foreign exchange, principally dollars, for Britain's overseas purchases and negotiating on these matters with the French. His personal enthusiasm for the war was not great; some of his closest friends, the Bloomsbury group, of which he was a slightly improbable member, were conscientious objectors. When he himself received a notice calling him to military service, he laid it aside as an error.

At Versailles in 1919, Keynes soon became disenchanted both with the leaders and with their decisions. On May 26, 1919, while the conference was still very much under way, he resigned from the British delegation and turned to the writing, for publication in a few months, of his assault on the whole misadventure. The book had an immediate, perhaps one may say incredible, impact. The memory of the effect when I first read it only a few years later is still with me.

Keynes's case, with no bow to understatement, was that

the Treaty had as its basic design, first, to ruin Germany and its capacity to pay and then to require payment. This departure from basic good sense he blamed squarely on the great leaders assembled at Versailles. Here he overstepped the unwritten convention of scholarly discourse, a convention that has already been mentioned and that still holds: one can attribute wrong motives to leaders; one can charge error; one cannot assert mere stupidity. This Keynes did: Woodrow Wilson he called 'this blind and deaf Don Quixote.'[3] Clemenceau, he said, 'had one illusion – France; and one disillusion – mankind.'[4] Lloyd George he called in an earlier draft 'this goat-footed bard, this half-human visitor to our age from the hag-ridden magic and enchanted woods of Celtic antiquity,'[5] but at the last moment he was persuaded, or perhaps persuaded himself, to substitute a slightly less fulsome characterization. Here is his more somber comment on the Treaty and the proceedings:

> The Treaty includes no provisions for the economic rehabilitation of Europe – nothing to make the defeated Central Empires into good neighbors, nothing to stabilize the new States of Europe, nothing to reclaim Russia; nor does it provide in any way a compact of economic solidarity amongst the Allies themselves; no arrangement was reached at Paris for restoring the disordered finances of France and Italy, or to adjust the systems of the Old World and the New.
> The Council of Four paid no attention to these issues. . . .

3. John Maynard Keynes, *Essays in Biography* (London: Mercury Books, 1961), p. 20.
4. Quoted in R. F. Harrod, *The Life of John Maynard Keynes* (London: Macmillan, 1954), p. 257.
5. Ibid., p. 256.

It is an extraordinary fact that the fundamental economic
problems of a Europe starving and disintegrating before
their eyes, was the one question in which it was impossible
to arouse the interest of the Four. Reparation was their
main excursion into the economic field, and they settled it
as a problem of theology, of politics, of electoral chicane,
from every point of view except that of the economic future
of the States whose destiny they were handling.[6]

The influence of The Economic Consequences extended
promptly and powerfully to all countries, and especially to
the United States. Some have attributed to the book Wilson's
defeat in the Congress on the League of Nations. There was
also bitter criticism: Keynes was charged with deserting his
country and the Allies and with yielding the peace to
Germany. He survived brilliantly; there is no doubt that the
prestige of any writer is considerably enhanced by being
proven right. Keynes's good fortune was to come out of the
world's misfortune.

In the next years Germany, having accepted the Treaty, made,
in fact, a rather determined effort to pay the assigned reparations. Her tax system was greatly strengthened; in the former
governmental structure the power to levy direct taxes had
been extensively reserved to the states.[7] Revenues could not,
however, keep up with demands, including those for the
exchange-stabilized marks with which reparations payments
had to be made. There was no alternative to borrowing, and
as time passed, this came to make up an ever-greater part of

6. Keynes, *Economic Consequences*, pp. 226–27.
7. See Graham, *Exchange, Prices, and Production*, pp. 36–37.

government expenditure. In consequence, prices rose and individuals abandoned bank accounts and savings in favor of the quick spending that protected against a loss of purchasing power.

Industrial and commercial holdings of cash or its equivalent were similarly converted into hard assets. This expenditure further enhanced the price increases; it also forced on the government more borrowing to meet *its* obligations. This borrowing had to be from the Reichsbank; no one wished to hold government bonds or other instruments with their rapidly decreasing purchasing power. There was also every advantage in delaying tax payments, for, as prices rose, money became more abundant and less valuable and so tax obligations could be paid off at a bargain rate. Yet more borrowing for needed public expenditure followed. In early 1923, to enforce, it was hoped, the terms of the Treaty, the French occupied the Ruhr. This, with the associated industrial collapse in Germany and the need to pay unemployment compensation, added to a cumulative process that was by now well under way on its own. The German inflation, which was to be the classic inflation of modern times, was fully on course.

Prices now rose by the day, soon by the hour. The only protection was to have not bank deposits but paper notes that could be quickly spent. All through 1923, it has been said, somewhere around half of the printing presses in Germany were printing money. Anyone who could exchange marks for foreign currency was obviously motivated to do so. In consequence, the exchange value of the mark fell even more dramatically than prices rose. In the summer of 1923, a United States congressman, A. P. Andrew, achieved a small footnote in history by receiving 4 billion marks in exchange for seven dollars, then paying 1.5 billion marks for a restaurant meal and giving a 400-million-mark tip.[8]

As the year passed, the situation became more extreme. Note issues of the Reichsbank had stood at 113.6 billion marks in December 1921. By December 1923, they had reached 496,507,424,800 billion marks.[9]

The larger effect of the inflation was a liquidation and transfer of wealth rivaling that in Russia in the same years. Holders of fixed or approximately fixed interest-bearing securities were wholly wiped out. So were those who otherwise depended on fixed or unresponsive income. Holders of real estate and industrial property in general were, in contrast, wonderfully enriched. There was, however, far more pain, overall, than pleasure. For the next seventy-five years, fully until our own time, the memory of the great inflation was to have a dominant influence on German economic policy.

At the end of 1923, in one of the more remarkable episodes in the history of money, the German inflation was brought to an end. A new currency, the rentenmark, came into being, and issuing and supporting it was a new bank, the Rentenbank. The new currency was, in an innovative way, held to be backed by the landed wealth of the new republic. Anyone mistrusting it could, in theory, turn it in for some good and solid real property. In fact, no one could; the backing was purely symbolic. But where money and its mystery are involved, it is open even to a government to perpetrate a

8. As told by Paul Johnson in *Modern Times: The World from the Twenties to the Eighties* (New York: Harper & Row, 1983), pp. 134–35.
9. Graham, *Exchange, Prices, and Production*, Table VII, p. 63.

benign fraud, which is what was done here. Because the government rigorously balanced its budget and refused to call on the bank for the loans that lie back of any money creation, the new currency, as evidenced by prices denoted therein, was wonderfully stable, and stability continued. It was another reason why so many people attributed magic to money.

Much of the credit for this operation, it should be noted, goes to Dr. Hjalmar Schacht, who headed the Reichsbank and forced the supporting austerity in government finance. He was embarked on a long path to world eminence, which ended in his greatly overpublicized economic service to Adolf Hitler. When he was called to answer at the Nuremberg trials after World War II, his wartime role was found also to be greatly inflated, perhaps not least by himself. He was acquitted. Members of my staff investigating the economic effects of the air attacks on Germany, of which I will later tell, found him an ill-informed, rather pathetic figure.

The further history of the reparations and inter-Allied debts can be briefly told. In the manner of the Latin American debts of our own day, they were subject to elaborate permutations, which had the principal effect of disguising the one solid fact that they could not or would not be paid. Paralleling the Baker Plan and the Brady Plan[10] on the Latin American debts of the 1980s were the Dawes Plan and the Young Plan on the German debt. In further parallel, the Dawes Plan loaned money to Germany to allow payment; some further payment

10. Named for two American Secretaries of the Treasury, these were plans that seemed to reduce the debts without actually doing so and vice versa.

came from a surprising boom in American loans to German cities, loans which also, more than incidentally, went eventually into default. Some of the German reparations were thus paid by American investors.

With the depression the charade came effectively to an end. In June 1931, Herbert Hoover offered a one-year moratorium on all reparations and inter-Allied debt payments. The following year a conference in Lausanne reduced reparations claims to a nearly nominal 3 billion marks. Adolf Hitler, coming to power in 1933, stopped all payments; at the end of the moratorium the British and French defaulted on their American debt, which left Finland in lonely if minute grandeur as the only country continuing to pay.

As with the enduring German attitude on inflation, so the experience here on both debt and reparations would have continuing effect. In World War II, Lend-Lease, really a free grant of funds, would replace international lending. As a major legacy of Keynes, reparations in money and the ensuing experience would be totally forsworn. Reparations henceforth would be in kind, physical industrial plant and again also coal. This would involve no intricate problem of cash or the balance of payments. Factories and machinery would simply be lifted and carried away to replace what had been destroyed in the invaded lands. As the State Department official primarily responsible for these matters in 1946, I would discover that this design, if pressed, could be at least as damaging a form of reparations after a war as payment in money.

Germany was not alone in suffering inflation, carefully called hyperinflation, after the Great War. Austria also suffered extreme inflation, which culminated in 1922. Presiding over it as Finance Minister at its beginning was the youthful economist Joseph Alois Schumpeter, later to be my teacher, colleague and friend. The Austrian experience, too, was of no slight consequence in later history; the economic views so formed would have a powerful effect on Schumpeter's economic thought and instruction in the next thirty years and on the considerable and responsive audience that he reached.

Nor would he be alone. Vienna before the war had more than a modest claim as the intellectual and cultural capital of the Old Europe. This clearly included its economists. The most influential of their number were, like Schumpeter, caught in the events of the time: along with inflation, the struggle between the socialists *cum* social democrats of Vienna, the conservative peasantry and what remained of the old ruling classes. All the economists, almost without exception, made their way west to Geneva, London and then on to the United States. Here, as the new arrivals from Vienna, they – Ludwig von Mises, Friedrich von Hayek, Fritz Machlup, Joseph Schumpeter – were to have influence, greater perhaps than they would have enjoyed in their own country. Theirs was part of a larger current of economic thought that strongly affected both public attitudes and, in some measure, public policy in the United States in the years following the Great War. These shaping ideas of the time are the subject of the next chapter.

5

The Economic Scene Then: A Digression

It was in the late 1920s that I first encountered formal economics as an influence that would shape my life. This was in the texts of Richard T. Ely, the leading economic figure of his time in the United States. Ely was the principal founder of the American Economic Association, my distant predecessor there as president, and was considered a liberal in the profession. His liberalism consisted predominantly in his nonacceptance of the Social Darwinism of William Graham Sumner, one of the most influential social voices of the late nineteenth century, who held, in early anticipation of Ronald Reagan, that the economic system rightly rewarded the rich for their contribution to general well-being and wisely punished the poor for their inadequacy. Going a step beyond the modern revival, Sumner also believed that the more than occasional euthanasia of the poor improved the race. I was no doubt fortunate that I did not fall under his influence.

My early instruction in economics was in Canada and was incidental to my larger study of agriculture in all its diverse requirements. It continued at the University of California at Berkeley, at first under the guidance of Ewald T. Grether, who remains a most distinguished member of that academic community.

I pause here to consider the lens through which one then saw the economic system. This is essential if one is to have a full or even an imperfect impression of the economic world of the time and that to come.

In Europe, the United States and, in substantial measure, Japan in the previous century, the economy had become, as it remains, a dual system. On one side, and strong in public perception, were the great firms, then largely led by the men or families who had founded them. Their names ranged from Krupp and Thyssen in Germany, to John Brown and Vickers in Britain, and on to Vanderbilt, Rockefeller, Morgan, Mellon, Harriman, Gary and Duke in the United States. The great business firm was still an expression of the personality of a dominant figure. The management-controlled firm, less pleasantly called the industrial bureaucracy, its leaders mostly and sometimes deservedly unknown, was still well in the future.

Complementing and, in the frequent case, sustaining the big enterprises was the other side – the thousands of small manufacturers, artisans, service enterprises, merchants and other entrepreneurs and the rural masses.

There was a clear view in economics as to the governing economic – and political – power. This, widely predominant, was the established classical view, soon to become with little depth of change the neoclassical view and in some manifestations properly called the classical faith. This was centered traditionally in England, especially at the University of Cambridge, where, in appreciation of Alfred Marshall (1842–1924), its most famous modern exponent, it was also called Marshallian economics. It was Marshall's *Principles* that I read, to some extent mastered and to a large extent accepted after arriving in California in 1931. The classical view had more distant origins in Adam Smith (1723–1790) and David Ricardo (1772–1823) and later in Vienna, where, in the last century, a remarkable assembly of scholars – the Austrian school of Friedrich von Wieser (1851–1926) and Eugen von Böhm-Bawerk (1851–1914), in company with an even more noted scholar, Karl Menger (1840–1921) – attracted world-wide interest and attention. Serious American students went to Vienna before the war. The general commitment to classical thought was, however, deep in the United States; in no other country was it so fully adopted as a guiding principle. So it was when I encountered it.

Classical economic thought, a thing of many refinements, held that economic activity was subject to its own inbuilt constraints, and these, by implication, also neutralized political power. If the economy worked automatically and well, there was no case for intrusion by the state.

The first of the classical concerns was the determination of price. This was accomplished impersonally by the competitive effort on the part of the producer to supply the sovereign and ultimately controlling consumer.

Production by the supplying firm was expanded to the point where additional sales threatened to involve higher costs than were covered by the price – in technical terms, to the point where marginal cost equaled price. Beyond that, additional production no longer added to earnings; rather, the higher costs at the stable price reduced return. As with one producer, so with all producers. From this came an equilibrium into which all producers settled. If the individual producer raised prices, all sales went to his competitors, and the cost and loss of the unsold product remained with him. To lower prices was to expand sales, but with costs exceeding the price and thus with a reduced return.

As consumer prices settled into this impersonal equilibrium, so, if somewhat less certainly, did the prices that make up the costs of production. Wages were at the level that attracted the last available worker, either untrained or with some required skill. If individually or collectively a higher wage was demanded or set, the worker or those so demanding did not get employment. Since they wanted and needed work, they would reduce their wage claim. Wages might become insufferably low. That was no one's fault; it was the labor market. In the more pleasant case of a labor shortage, competition would bid up wages to a new equilibrium level, and prices would be forced up in a compensatory way.

The case was the same with the price of capital – the rate of interest. This was also set competitively at levels reflecting the supply of savings. With more savings available, the rate of interest would fall, and investment opportunities that were hitherto unprofitable would now become attractive. A new equilibrium would be established, and this would occur, as ever, in the impersonal manner of the market. If the rate of interest was too high, funds available for investment would fail to find employment, and rates would come down.

Finally there was profit. If this was high, competitors would promptly be attracted. If low, entrepreneurs, small and large, would reduce or abandon investment. From this would come a prevailing rate of profit. This too, some differences in energy and intelligence apart, was beyond the power of any one producing firm to control.

There was, as noted, a near infinity of refinements of this system. They were what sustained economic discussion and more sophisticated instruction and provided the subject matter for scholarly journals. It is not clear that anyone accepted all of this system; Christian faith does not require a literal acceptance of everything in the Holy Scripture. A certain measure of well-expressed qualification, even doubt, was normal. Over all was the covering justification.

In broad accepted tendency, this system took authority away from the individual firm, and especially from its ownership interest. Much as he (or very rarely she) might be so disposed, the owner was restrained by competitive and market forces from exploiting his consumers, his suppliers or his workers. If any of the latter suffered, it was from the natural order of things. Similarly, if the employer was affluent, even ostentatiously so, thus he was meant to be.

The political power of the owner was also constrained. Prices, production, wages, other outlays and profits were set by the market, and since they were thus controlled, there was no need or role for state intervention. There was little else to be asked for from the state except national defense, some public works, the post office, low taxes and the prevention of forthright fraud.

More generally, there was the matter of motivation. A dark day awaited the businessman who did not pay attention to business. The landed proprietor had had the leisure for, and the obligation to, a more spacious public participation, and that had been his natural and inherited duty. A businessman, in contrast, had to stick to his knitting.

*

The controlling role of classical economics and the market was never quite as pure, quite as precise, in Europe as in the United States. But in the United States too there were always doubts as to its total benignity. As early as 1866, Massachusetts took the lead in protecting some of its citizens from a too rigorous exposure to the market. In that year the Massachusetts legislature made history by enacting a law limiting the labor of children *under fourteen* to eight hours a day.[1] In Europe the legal constraints on the market were rather more comprehensive. In Germany in the 1880s, at the behest of Count Otto von Bismarck, legislation was passed providing a compulsory health insurance program and requiring support for workers afflicted by accident, sickness, old age or other disability. Similar action followed elsewhere in Europe, and particularly in Britain, where from 1908 to 1911, under the sponsorship of Lloyd George, insurance was provided first against the incapacities of old age, then against unemployment and finally against illness.

In Germany, France and, in lesser measure, Britain, a sophisticated working class was not impressed by the classical neutralization of power. Authority was held extensively to reside with the owner of the enterprise – the capitalist. Marx (and the other socialist writers) were read, taught and widely discussed. Even during World War I, while most workers were caught up either by force or by strong nationalist sentiment in the enthusiasm of war, there were still reservations. Lenin, spending these years in a scholarly way in

---

1. See Ernest Ludlow Bogart, *Economic History of the American People* (New York: Longmans, Green and Co., 1930), p. 620.

Switzerland, convened conferences – one at Zimmerwald near Bern in 1915, another the following spring at Kiental – to condemn the conflict as a capitalist assault on the working class. A certain and justified caution characterized these meetings; the one at Zimmerwald was ostensibly a gathering of bird watchers. For possessing or disseminating this working-class view of the war as it emerged from Kiental and found its way to the trenches of the Western Front, two German officers and thirty-two privates were therapeutically shot.

In Europe to this day, as also in Japan, there is still the lurking notion that the state is in the service of the economy – of the capitalist system. In Marx's words, it is the executive committee of the capitalist classes. One of the curiosities of modern economic history is that countries where the young read Marx, the most obvious case being Japan, have in recent times had a stronger economic performance than those that are still subject to the classical rules that exclude the state and the union from any substantive role because the economy is systemically self-ruling.

This, however, runs ahead of the story. The classical ideas as one encountered them in the 1920s and 1930s in the United States call for another word.

If in Europe there was a certain ambiguity as to the power of the capitalist and the role of the state, in the United States there was less or none. Here, for both those who had accorded it formal study and those for whom it was part of the political atmosphere, the classical system ruled. But it did so with one greatly plausible exception.

That, not surprisingly, was where there was no competition. Competition, the prices set impersonally by the market, was the decisive force in maintaining the benign equilibrium. In its absence – with monopoly – the whole social justification for the system was, to say the least, at risk. This led inexorably to the further conclusion: if there is monopoly, the state must limit its power – either dissolve or regulate it. The classical system not only allowed state intervention to this end but in a very real sense demanded it. Natural monopolies such as rail transportation, electrical transmission and telephonic communication would have to be subject to regulation or public ownership and operation. Other monopolies would have to be disallowed, broken up.

Already, beginning in 1890 with the Sherman Anti-Trust Act of that year,[2] the Congress had taken steps to outlaw this theoretically indefensible impairment of the classical system. In 1914, supplementary legislation followed – the Clayton Act and the Federal Trade Commission Act, both passed during the Wilson administration. Though restrained as to application by the courts, including by the Supreme Court, the antimonopoly legislation became a fixed feature of American economic history. Even by conservatives monopoly could not systemically be defended. Antitrust action could be greatly disliked, but its deeper logic had to be accepted. Aversion was somewhat mitigated by the fact that, unexpectedly but quite plausibly, considering the controlling doctrine, trade unions were highly visible antitrust offenders and were so seen by the courts.

2. They were called 'trusts' because individual owners of two or several companies surrendered their stock for trust certificates that gave them the welcome pecuniary reward from participation in the better revenues of the thus-created monopoly.

For liberals in this time the antitrust laws were a comprehensive economic therapy. Given any evident misuse of market power, more broadly any defective economic performance, the answer was clear: enforce the antitrust laws. This, then and later, became, on frequent occasion, the ready recourse of the devoid liberal mind.

The larger point must be emphasized: in the United States in the 1920s and extending on to later times, the classical system was the controlling force in the economy for both the left and the right. So it was on my first introduction to the subject of economics.

The situation, as I've indicated, was different in Europe and later in Japan. There the classical system, or certainly its antitrust therapy, had no similar force. Monopoly, including the great cartels, was accepted. Adverse legislation was seen, not unreasonably, as outlawing the very system itself. These attitudes were sharply in conflict with American belief. In the years of the American occupation of Germany after World War II, one of the major economic reforms pressed by the United States on the new German state was an antitrust law. At the same time in Japan steps (soon reversed) were taken to break up, dissolve, the great industrial complexes, the *zaibatsu*. This, it was thought, would lead toward democracy; it would also contribute in a friendly way to better operation of the economic system in the future. The classical rules were not a purely American design; they were taken to have universal application and effect.

In time, the concern for monopoly would diminish, as also the support for antitrust therapy. Beginning in the 1930s, there was the intrusion on the classical system of the idea of imperfect or oligopolistic competition. Not one but a few firms in tacit understanding, one with the other, might have the same influence on prices and production as a single producer. Oligopoly instead of monopoly. And perhaps because of advertising, other public-relations persuasion, even location, the producer might so differentiate his product as to enjoy an appreciable and recognizable command over price. Monopolistic competition. Monopoly in greater or lesser power was thus made not special but general, and it did not seem entirely practical to outlaw the whole or nearly the whole industrial system. There was also the rise of foreign competition. No one could much worry about monopoly in American markets when similar Japanese products were wonderfully available.

It came to be seen as well that as regards the modern great and often bureaucratic corporation there was more to be feared from incompetence than from market power.

Finally, in recent times, there was the highly selective restriction on the role of the state. In the 1980s, this went so far as to encompass the antitrust laws. These were not repealed; they were simply not enforced. This was, save by the lawyers involved, one of the less noticed developments of the Reagan years.

However, this occurs later in my journey. In the 1920s and early 1930s, all of this was yet to come. My own introduction, to repeat, was to a system in which competition was a benign and nearly universal force and regulator.

There was a little more. In the United States and elsewhere in the 1920s, university instruction was given on money and banking and on the business cycle. The gold standard was assumed to be normal; different national currencies exchanged with each other and with gold at fixed rates. Or such was the expectation. Taken for granted in the industrial countries, in effect, was an approximation to the single currency toward which the European states now, in the 1990s, are struggling. A prime function of the central banks and of government fiscal policy, taxation and expenditure was to sustain this stability in international exchange relationships, a matter we will take up again.

Fluctuations in business activity, business cycles, were also course material in the universities. They were variously explained. Until slightly earlier times reputable observers had attributed them, through variations in agricultural crop yields or more exotic influences, to sun spots. Joseph Schumpeter spoke of 'the perennial gale of creative destruction' by which the established and the senile were swept aside and the way was thus cleared for new and greater achievements to come. Speculative orgies were held to have something to do with this phenomenon. So was war and its aftermath. Overall, however, there remained the classical commitment to full employment, the normal condition to which the system was returned by basic economic forces. To the onslaught on this system, less by scholarship than by events, I now turn.

6

Portents

As compared with what went before or what came after, the 1920s are thought by historians to have been a time of calm in the United States. For most of those years Calvin Coolidge was in the White House; few Presidents have been less given to disturbing initiatives. Economic life was good by the conventional measures; in a distant preview of the 1980s, Secretary of the Treasury Andrew Mellon, himself a man of wealth and therefore a significant beneficiary of his own action, reduced taxes. It was not then thought necessary to offer (or, more precisely, invent) a solemn economic justification. To have lower taxes was enough.

Although I had my first introduction to the study of economics at the end of the 1920s, I did not reflect much on the current condition. Things seemed either intensely normal or unworthy of youthful interest. Eventually, however, my attention was to be drawn strongly to this decade, and a quarter of a century later I came, as I've earlier indicated, to write a history of the great stock market debacle of 1929.[1] I

1. *The Great Crash, 1929* (Boston: Houghton Mifflin, 1955). Later citations in this book are to the edition published by Houghton Mifflin in 1988.

focused especially on the 1920s in the United States, as somewhat earlier study had involved me in the British experience of that same decade. I here, on occasion, retrieve what I've said before. To the British experience I come presently, but first a word on the general economic scene.

The 1920s were not a time of universal well-being. In Germany and the remnants of the old Austro-Hungarian Empire there was the limitless inflation already described. After that came regressive and depressive economic conditions as government expenditures were brought within the limits of revenues, and the associated bank borrowing and currency creation were brought to an end. In Germany this commitment to rigorously orthodox finance was to extend into the 1930s under Chancellor Heinrich Brüning and make even more painful the Great Depression. (Brüning was presently to be invited to Harvard as a member of the Department of Government. Some students and young faculty members, of whom I was one, thought a more exciting possibility would have been King Zog of Albania, who had been recently expelled from his country.)

Democracy would come to be seen in Germany as the parent of hardship, as already it had been so seen in Italy. From this would come the Axis dictatorships in those two countries and the acceptance of repressive government, at least partly as the seeming price of a tolerable level of economic well-being.

The 1920s were not a good time in Britain either. In 1920 and 1921, as wartime shortages were overcome and the budget was brought back toward balance, wartime inflation tapered to an end. There followed perhaps the single most damaging error of modern economic and financial policy – a hard competition to win. It was the decision taken by the British Chancellor of the Exchequer to return the country to the gold standard at the old gold content of the pound, 123.27 grains of fine gold, and to the old exchange rate of $4.87 to the pound. This meant a wonderfully prompt appreciation of the pound in relation to gold and to the dollar. It was expected that this would cause individuals of questionable faith to exchange their sterling for the now suddenly less expensive dollars or gold, and to cover this possibility, supporting funds were obtained by the Bank of England from the Federal Reserve Bank of New York and from J. P. Morgan – $200 million and $100 million respectively.

The Chancellor was Winston Churchill, his political career now redeemed. Speaking to the House of Commons on April 28, 1925, he said in superb Churchillian metaphor that henceforth the nations of the British Commonwealth and the world as a whole would be united by the gold standard and would 'vary together, like ships in harbor whose gangways are joined and who rise and fall together with the tide.' The press response was all he could have wished. The *New York Times* told next day that 'according to [the] opinion expressed in the lobby,' the speech was one of the 'finest in a long line'; the *Times* headline said that Churchill's announcement had carried 'PARLIAMENT AND NATION TO HEIGHT OF ENTHUSI-ASM.'[2] The more sober reality was a major social and political disaster.

The disastrous truth was that, reflecting still the wartime

2. *New York Times*, April 29, 1925.

price increases, British exports were far too costly in the dollars, gold or other currencies now required to buy the pounds and thus the products. If used elsewhere, the same dollars or gold could buy more coal or manufactured goods. The only solution, given the importance to Britain of exports (and imports purchased therefrom), was for the British prices to come down – and to this end also the wages that, as in the case of the coal industry, comprised much of those prices. Resisting the wage reduction, there was a strike in the coal pits, labor troubles elsewhere and then the angry General Strike. There followed a period of economic stagnation and unemployment that extended over the decade. Rarely, to repeat, has a single economic decision had such an unhappy effect.

Ten years before, as earlier told, Winston Churchill had initiated the military action at the Dardanelles, the most spectacular military error of World War I; now on economics and finance he had equally excelled. He would later and brilliantly recover. No politician of modern times has rivaled Churchill's ability to go back and forth from desolate error to major success.

In this instance he was helped, in a manner of speaking, by John Maynard Keynes, to whom, once again, economists are indebted for the clear view. The error, Keynes explained, was made by the high and presumptively informed civil servants of the Treasury and of the larger financial community in the City. Nothing, in their opinion, could be more important than restoring the pound to its nineteenth-century integrity and preeminence. Speaking of Churchill, Keynes said in a kindly way that he had 'no instinctive judgment to prevent him from making [such] mistakes' and, lacking it, he 'was deafened by the clamorous voices of conventional finance.'[3] In Britain the Great Depression of the 1930s was a grave and painful thing. In contrast to the depression in the United States, however, it followed upon dreary years of economic stagnation, unemployment and unrest.

The contrast between Britain and the United States in the 1920s could not, indeed, have been more striking: between 1914 and 1920, the gold reserves of the United States had increased from $1.8 billion to $2.8 billion. The approximate doubling of prices during the war years had left the country, as was the case elsewhere, with the already noticed memory of inflation – one that was strongly influential twenty years later as World War II approached. In 1920, however, prices leveled off. There was a slight depression – always then the mildest possible term. The economy then stabilized and improved. From a great inflow of hard money came the funds for borrowing and investment. This continued at a high level during the decade, as did economic activity in general. Between 1925 and 1929, the number of manufacturing establishments increased from 183,877 to 206,663; the value of their output rose from $60,809,225,000 to $67,994,041,000.[4] 'The Federal Reserve index of industrial production which had averaged only 67 in 1921 (1923–25 = 100) had risen to 110 by July 1928, and it reached 126 in June 1929. In 1926, 4,301,000 automobiles were produced. Three years later, in 1929, production had increased by over

3. John Maynard Keynes, *Essays in Persuasion* (New York: Harcourt, Brace and Co., 1932), p. 246.
4. *Statistical Abstract of the United States, 1944–45* (U.S. Department of Commerce, Bureau of the Census), Table 893, p. 794.

a million to 5,358,000.'⁵ Earnings were rising rapidly; it was a very good time to be in business.

But money was available for more than the purchase of automobiles. It was also wonderfully available to finance the hope of making more money – for speculation.

Speculation begins when a price is going up and the presumptively wise expect a further increase. They buy and thus produce the increase. More buy, and more and yet more are attracted. Each price increase affirms the good sense of those who have bought before. Those who doubt are reviled as creatures of defective imagination. The buying and the supporting mood continue until the available supply of mentally vulnerable, economically viable buyers is exhausted. Then come the changed view of the prospect, the rush to get out, the pressure now of creditors demanding repayment of the loans that financed purchase, thus forcing sale. In short, the crash.

Other features are constant and have been over the centuries since the great tulip speculation in Holland in the seventeenth century. One is the seeming miracle of leverage. If money is borrowed with a fixed interest return to make an investment, all the gain from the increased price will accrue, and in multiple amount, to the borrower.

It is also thought that those who, with leverage, are riding the boom are endowed with a fresh and persuasive genius. They and their financial acuity are the wonder of the time. After the crash the sad truth is revealed: they were vulnerable individuals caught by their own fantasy. Not rarely, this

5. Galbraith, *The Great Crash*, p. 2.

fantasy is found to have carried them beyond the law. The last chapter in the life of the financial genius tells of intense public disapprobation and frequently of his consignment to exile or a substantial term in a relatively benign but still far from agreeable jail.

Finally there is the search, in which economists are known to participate in a cooperative way, to find some external reason for the bursting of the speculative bubble. It is almost never supposed that in a rational world the speculation contains the seeds of its own destruction; something else, some outside development or event, must have brought it to an end.

In the United States in the 1920s, the speculative mood that strongly characterized that decade was first made manifest in the geographically rather restricted Florida land boom.

Based on the undoubted fact that the winter climate in Florida is better than that in Minneapolis or even New York, there came, in the early years of the decade, a vision of unlimited riches from the ownership of land under the favoring winter sun. So streets were laid out, and the adjacent, often unruly acreage was divided into lots. Somewhat imaginatively, properties were described as at the seashore when they were ten or fifteen miles from the nearest salt water. This mattered little because most of those buying had little thought of taking up residence themselves. Having made a 10 percent down payment, they awaited the always welcome effect of leverage that would come with resale and result in a modest doubling or thereabouts of the previous price. After the debt was repaid, there would be a tenfold gain, more or less, on the original investment. From across the country a wave of profit seekers descended on Florida, some by train, some by automobile. So great was the traffic that eventually the railroads were forced to place an embargo on the unnecessary movement of freight, including building materials. (The latter, one could only suppose, were not irrelevant to the development of the real estate.) In Miami salesmen stood out on the streets to greet the new arrivals and offer them property there on the spot. Why not buy now; it will be worth as much again a few weeks hence. Unasked was the question as to why the seller did not keep the land and the profit for himself.

The boom spread north. As it approached Jacksonville, it attracted the efforts of no less a figure than Charles Ponzi. Only a few years earlier he had aroused Boston from its refined torpor with an investment company of highly uncertain purpose that provided rich profits to early investors from the capital supplied by later gulls. Ever since, this has been known as the Ponzi scheme. Ponzi's subdivision 'near Jacksonville' had an especially larcenous base. It was, in fact, approximately sixty-five miles from the city. No land, however, was wasted; twenty-three building sites were marked out to every acre. His genius was to see that people who believe they are singled out to be rich are always available for fiscal suicide, however obvious its inevitability.

Soon the end came, as it always does. In 1926, the supply of new buyers ran out. The boom tapered off; land prices stabilized and went down. Then came the events which, for some, lent seeming rationality to the collapse. That autumn two hurricanes blew in from the mild waters to the south. Prices went down disastrously. The winds were blamed for what would have occurred in any case. Some land, having passed through the hands of a half-dozen speculators, each reaping the rewards of leverage, was returned in successive defaults to the original owner. It now had sidewalks, street lamps and tax assessments amounting to several times its current value. In 1925, bank clearings in Miami were $1,066,528,000. By 1928, they were down to a mere $143,364,000.[6]

The Florida boom was a small window on the speculative atmosphere of the time. The 1920s were the early affirmation that this was, indeed, the American century. The larger national mood would be given voice many times, and not exclusively by politicians. There was, however, no better political expression of it than President Calvin Coolidge's last message to the Congress on December 4, 1928. 'No Congress of the United States ever assembled,' he said, 'on surveying the state of the Union, has met with a more pleasing prospect than that which appears at the present time. In the domestic field there is tranquillity and contentment . . . and the highest record of years of prosperity.' After noting that abroad there was peace and 'the good will which comes from mutual understanding,' he told his audience that they and the country could 'regard the present with satisfaction and anti-cipate the future with optimism.'[7]

The President was here reflecting two tendencies that recur in our official discourse. One is to regard anything that is good as permanent, a fully deserved feature of the American polity. And he made that explicit: 'The main source of these

6. Frederick Lewis Allen, *Only Yesterday* (New York: Harper, 1931), p. 282.
7. *The Congressional Record*, 70th Congress, 2nd Session, Part 1, p. 20.

unexampled blessings lies in the integrity and character of the American people.'[8]

The second tendency is to say, and more often than not to believe, that what is good for the more fortunate of the populace must, *per se*, be good for all. Mr. Coolidge in his eloquent statement addressed only the financially well-endowed, a small minority of the population at the time. Ordinary workers were then putting in long hours for low pay, and most were denied any protection by unions. It was considered their good fortune that they could receive the very limited well-being that derived from the goodwill of those whom a steel magnate of a slightly earlier generation had called 'the worthy men to whom God in his wisdom had entrusted the industrial life of the country.'

Minorities, blacks in particular, were, as a matter of course, excluded from effective participation in the national good fortune; they toiled on southern plantations in circumstances not appreciably different from those in the days before the Civil War. The feudal structure remained. Women and children were unprotected from the crudest of exploitation.

Agriculture, still a centrally important part of the economy, was a special area of discontent. Competing with undifferentiated products in purely competitive markets with costs and prices that none controlled, farmers represented the closest approach to the classical ideal of the economic system. They were also, of all producers, the most at odds *with* the system. In the years to come, the administration of Herbert Hoover would invest millions of dollars through the Federal Farm Board in a futile but not wholly implausible effort to give

8. Ibid.

farmers, by way of cooperatives, some of the bargaining power that was enjoyed by those who sold them equipment, fertilizer or other supplies or who bought their crops and livestock.

None of this was a matter of central concern in the formal and reputable economics of the time. Because of my rural background and my study of agricultural matters in general and agricultural economics in particular, it was soon to enter my own thinking. But for those economists committed to the previously mentioned classical design, it was a special case well outside their field. It was 'the farm problem.' That the classical system in its most nearly perfect form could be associated with grave discontent and hardship was largely ignored.

Nor was the dim, dismal or unrewarding life still lived by many a generally recognized fact in the 1920s. The comfortable simply assumed their situation extended to all. And this view was articulated for them by Calvin Coolidge. As with Ronald Reagan a half century on, innocence forgave error. Even while Coolidge addressed the Congress, however, the economic forces that would strip his words of their authority and, indeed, change them to an historical amusement were well advanced. The great Wall Street speculation was strongly under way.

7

The Crash

The Wall Street boom of the 1920s, the economic symbol and centerpiece of that decade in the United States and an undoubted source of much of the sorrow and distress that followed, was no sudden thing. It began slowly in 1924, continued in 1925, suffered a minor setback in 1926, perhaps as a distant reflection of the Florida real estate collapse, and then began in earnest in 1927. It continued strongly in 1928, and after a momentary break in March of 1929, on which a later word, it went into a culminating ascent in the summer months of that year. In September there was a sharp drop, and in the ensuing weeks there was a mood of uncertainty – days of optimism followed by days of doubt. Then on Thursday, October 24, and powerfully on the following Tuesday, came the crash.

Of this, as I've said, I wrote nearly forty years ago, recapturing scenes of my youth and realizing, on occasion, how far from complete was my earlier perception. Of the various economic matters that have attracted or required my interest over the years, none ever became more compelling than the crash and the preceding speculation. It was an episode wonderful in its delirium but not less in its drama and tragedy. And tragedy, as I've elsewhere observed, can be quietly enjoyed when, as is not true of war, nothing is being lost but money. I recall my research and writing of *The Great Crash* as a time of nearly undiluted pleasure.

No less delight came from its appearance, if briefly, on the bestseller lists, my first entry into that reasonably rewarding and, one hopes, also distinguished company. Succeeding episodes of speculation and disaster, large and small, have, as I've indicated, kept the book in print during the years since. An author should choose his subjects with discretion and care, with special attention to history that will repeat itself.

I learned also from the writing of this book, as I've often told, of the need for care as to a title, even when the selection seems of the most direct and plausible sort. Some time after the volume first appeared in the mid-1950s, on one of my frequent trips to New York I was walking by a small bookshop in the old La Guardia air terminal early one evening. I paused as usual to see if the book was in the window. It was not, and having time on my hands, I went into the store in a casual way, ostensibly to browse. The woman behind the counter, however, sought me out to ask if I was looking for something special; embarrassed, I mumbled the author's name, 'something like Galbraith,' and then more strongly articulated the title, '*The Great Crash*.'

'That isn't a book you could sell in an airport,' she said firmly.

There was perhaps deeper instruction from observing how the boom that preceded the crash reflected the mood of the time and how closely the crash conformed to and highly dramatized the rules governing such episodes.

*

As to the national mood, there was the picture of great, enduring and deserved prosperity so admirably articulated by President Coolidge. Sustaining it was the vision of a new world of industry and technology, dominated by automobile manufacture with its still widely admired assembly lines and, especially, by the new communications world of radio. The speculative favorite of those years was RCA, the Radio Corporation of America. Its future was, indeed, before it; RCA had never paid a dividend.

In keeping with this mood and justified by it was, as ever, the self-sustaining power of the speculative boom. As with the Florida acreage, the improving prices of stocks brought in the buyers who bought and sent prices still higher, thus supporting in a very persuasive way their previous decision to buy.

This tendency was strongly augmented in the late 1920s by numerous craftsmen who, having a broad general understanding of the process, joined to bid up the price of a particular stock and engage in promiscuous buying and selling to draw attention thereto. Having thus attracted the participation and money of the innocent, the avaricious and the gullible, they sold out at the considerably improved price. This was the speculative pool. Unusually adept in this exercise, and famous for it because of his own later advertisement of the operation, was Joseph P. Kennedy, father of a future President and founder and financial support of what would be the nation's most celebrated family in the twentieth century. Unlike others, he detached himself in time and was not, as was normal, the victim of his own presumed financial acumen.

Present also, as never before and indeed not since, was

leverage. This was available in simple form in the purchase of stocks on margin – a down payment with the rest borrowed from the broker, who borrowed, in turn, from the banks. All the increase in value then accrued to the borrowing stockholder. There were elements of caution here, however; most borrowers were required to put up 45 or 50 percent of the purchase price.

In the end, that would turn out to be not nearly enough. When the crash came, there followed calls for more margin from individuals who could not come up with the cash. The resulting sales added dramatically to the pressures provoking the downward plunge and, needless to say, to the grave distress of other speculators, leveraged or not.

There was, however, a more sophisticated kind of leverage – more precisely, double, triple and quadruple leverage and even more. Its most admired manifestation was in the closed-end investment trusts, companies organized for the sole purpose of buying, holding and trading in securities. To this end, in the great years of the twenties, these trusts issued stock, bonds and preferred stock. The bonds and preferred stock with fixed return did not rise with the price of the purchased stock. All the gains therefrom accrued to the value of the common stock of the purchasing company. This was primary leverage. The next step was to have the company so created promote yet another company to buy stock. Bonds and preferred stock as well as common stock were issued by this new company. The gains from the increasing value of the common stock of the company so launched accrued exclusively to the promoting company's common stock. That stock in wonderfully enhanced value went on to increase substantially the value of the common stock of the parent company. These structures could be several stories high.

The most famous example of this leverage was created by Goldman, Sachs and Company, which, in late 1928, organized the Goldman Sachs Trading Corporation. Its only reason for being was to own stock in other companies; to do this, it issued securities amounting to $100 million, around a billion dollars in today's prices. There were no bonds or preferred stock; leverage was not yet involved. That oversight was, however, quickly corrected. The Trading Corporation organized the Shenandoah Corporation with common stock and preferred stock, the latter with a fixed return. The initial issue was $102.5 million, and it was said to have been oversubscribed by some sevenfold.

Control remained with the Goldman Sachs Trading Corporation and with the parent Goldman, Sachs, as was the case with an even greater enterprise, the Blue Ridge Corporation, which was sponsored, in turn, by Shenandoah with capital of $142 million. The large gains in the common stock of Blue Ridge as its holdings boomed went in powerful concentration to the common stock of Shenandoah and by multiples from Shenandoah on to the Trading Corporation. The financial world marveled. So, without doubt, did one of the directors, who was to be of later fame, Mr. John Foster Dulles. Missing only was the yet-to-be-discovered fact that leverage could go viciously into reverse.

On this there was a revealing footnote a few years later in Washington. It occurred at a congressional hearing on the unfortunate aftermath of the crash and the reverse power of leverage:

SENATOR COUZENS [a liberal Michigan Republican]: Did Goldman, Sachs and Company organize the Goldman Sachs Trading Corporation?

MR. SACHS: Yes, sir.

SENATOR COUZENS: And it sold its stock to the public?

MR. SACHS: A portion of it. The firm invested originally in 10 per cent of the entire issue for the sum of $10,000,000.

SENATOR COUZENS: And the other 90 per cent was sold to the public?

MR. SACHS: Yes, sir.

SENATOR COUZENS: At what price?

MR. SACHS: At 104. That is the old stock . . . the stock was split two for one.

SENATOR COUZENS: And what is the price of the stock now?

MR. SACHS: Approximately 1 and $\frac{3}{4}$.[1]

Such was leverage in reverse. There were many other examples of closed-end trusts, some even more spacious in scale and imagination. All went down with multiple effect.

Leverage was also used to buy railroads and utilities. The design was basically the same. From Cleveland the Van Sweringen brothers controlled a huge railroad empire with a nearly minuscule investment. From Chicago Samuel Insull presided over a great midwestern utility complex, which, as I've elsewhere said, he could not possibly have understood. There were numerous other such adventures. For all, reverse leverage awaited.

It would have been hard, indeed, to identify a more disastrously vulnerable design or one better calculated to

1. *Stock Exchange Practices*, Hearings, April–June 1932, Part 2, pp. 566–67, quoted in Galbraith, *The Great Crash*, pp. 69–70.

make worse the panic when it came. The world of high finance can be understood only when it is recognized that the greatest admiration is accorded those who are paving the way for the greatest catastrophe.

The question arises as to why something was not done. Was everyone gulled? Could not the Federal Reserve have clamped down on the credit that was so generously financing the purchase of stock? That thought did occur. In March 1929, there were persistent rumors that the Federal Reserve, then a little more than fifteen years old and combining incompetence with inconsequence, might take action thus to limit the supply of credit available for the purchase of securities, although it was far from clear how this would be accomplished. The market weakened, but it quickly recovered when, in a monumental exercise in arrogance, Charles E. Mitchell, the head of the National City Bank, as it then was, promised to offset with loans from his bank any adverse effect of Federal Reserve action. Of the latter there was none, and the market soared on.

The danger from the speculative mood and its eventual collapse, it might be noted, was urged by Paul M. Warburg, one of the founders of the Federal Reserve and, by later consent, the most intelligent Wall Street figure of his time. He spoke of the current orgy of 'unrestrained speculation' and said that were it not brought to a halt, there would be a disastrous collapse that would 'bring about a general depression involving the entire country.'[2] He was promptly accused of 'sandbagging American prosperity.' Some sus-

2. *The Commercial and Financial Chronicle*, March 9, 1929, p. 1444.

pected him of being short in the market.[3] Anti-Semitism was only slightly below the surface. I cite the Warburg prediction with some pleasure because for thirty-five years, as professor and professor emeritus, I have held the academic chair at Harvard that bears his name.

Reverse leverage of a personal sort extended disagreeably to those who were most celebrated in the boom. Samuel Insull, just mentioned, went to Greece when his utility complex collapsed, but in time he returned to face trial for alleged misfeasance. After his eventual acquittal, he was little heard of again. Ivar Kreuger, the most famous of the international speculators, an exponent of the forged as well as what was later to be called the junk bond, went out one evening in Paris, bought a gun and returned to his lodgings, where the next morning he shot himself. To avoid an adverse effect on the now-depressed markets, the news of his death was held up until trading was over for the day.

Similar response to the new adversity was not exceptional, although the press and black humor almost certainly exaggerated the effect. Hotel clerks did not ask incoming guests whether the room was for sleeping or jumping; the oft-told report that two market operatives had joined hands and jumped because they had a joint account is distinctly unlikely. There were for many, however, dark clouds of sorrow and personal ruin.

The stress and distress extended to the great bankers of the day. On Black Thursday (October 24, 1929), the first day of the disaster, the heads of the Chase, National City, Bankers

3. See Galbraith, *The Great Crash*, p. 72.

Trust and Guaranty Trust met at the offices of J. P. Morgan to consider what might be done. Previously, as the market weakened, there had been reassuring word that if things should turn bad, the bankers would step in; in the language of the day, there would be organized support. Now there was. Richard Whitney, the Vice President of the New York Stock Exchange at the time and brother of a leading Morgan partner, appeared presently on the floor of the Exchange to make a series of highly ostentatious purchases. This and the reports of the earlier meeting – the bankers had been seen assembling – changed the mood dramatically. The fall was arrested; the speculative favorites rebounded. Alas, it didn't last. The following Tuesday, a day of total desperation, there was a rumor that the bankers were selling off the securities they had bought in support of the market. Whether it was true or not, their reputation as a sustaining force suffered. The market continued down.

Others were less fortunate. Richard Whitney, after bringing about the welcome reversal on Black Thursday, was rewarded in ensuing months with the presidency of the Exchange. Then, abruptly one day, he was arrested and sent to prison for stealing funds from his customers' accounts and those of the Stock Exchange with which he had been entrusted.

The heads of the two largest American banks, National City and Chase, were also washed away with the tide. Charles Mitchell of National City, who earlier had defended the market against the possibly nonexistent threat of Federal Reserve action, was himself heavily involved. Seeking a loss for income tax purposes (as he admitted), he sold stock after the crash to his unknowing and possibly unsuspecting wife. Months of unpleasant litigation followed. Although he was ultimately held to be innocent, his great days were over.

Albert H. Wiggin, head of the Chase, was found to be short in the stock of his own bank at the time of the crash, meaning that, quite shrewdly, he was gambling on the chance that it would do badly, which it did. This was not thought to be a constructive pursuit for one who was variously President, Chairman of the Board and Chairman of the Governing Board of the institution. Wiggin said, nonetheless, that the short selling demonstrated his keen personal interest in the affairs of his employer. He was retired with a lifetime salary of $100,000, about a million dollars at today's prices, which, on examination, turned out to be his own thoughtful gift to himself.

A bevy of large but lesser figures – Bernard E. ('Sell 'em Ben') Smith; M. J. Meehan, an especially admired trader; Arthur W. Cutten, a Canadian come with high visibility to the world of Wall Street; Harry F. Sinclair, the already well-known oil executive; and others – were called before Congress to explain their operations and especially their varied efforts at market rigging. They proved an unprepossessing lot. Meehan absentmindedly went abroad when called to Washington but later returned and apologized for his carelessness. Cutten suffered from a severe loss of memory, as did some of the others. Sinclair had previously been in jail for Teapot Dome derelictions, although this, it appeared, had not interfered with his stock market operations. It was hard to believe that such a commonplace group had been the heroes of the time. There would be a similar wonder about similar financial figures as the 1980s ended.

*

There is always pleasure in the fall of the great and the greatly fraudulent. It shows that there is an inherent justice in the system. The more spectacular the previous aberration and social damage, the more spectacular now the fall, and this can be viewed with a certain mean approval. But there is also the larger fact elsewhere mentioned. It is that most people, living in modest circumstances as they do, have a magnified impression of the intelligence of those who live in intimate association with large sums of money. Surely, if they have so much, they must be exceptional. Handling it with insouciant casualness in the manner of speculators and some of the great bankers, they must, it can only be assumed, have a special talent, a deeper perception of the way the economic world works. This is an unusually erroneous belief, as the ultimate reckoning so reliably reveals. They are, in fact, the instrument not of their own intelligence but of their illusions.

I turn now to the aftermath of the crash, to the economic attitudes that were then shaped and that are vibrantly alive to the present day and to the lessons that were then learned and have since been grievously unlearned.

8

The Great Depression

Economics as a subject matter is normally lacking in drama; change for better or worse is incremental and often discovered in a scholarly way only after the fact. It is identification of this gradual process, its origins and its flow that accords economists much of their professional reputation. The year 1929 and the events of that unhappy October were in marked contrast with this orderly, even subtle tendency; after the stock market crash came the Great Depression. This was to last a full ten years and extend to all the industrial world. It was eased by public policy, of which more later, but it was ended only by the different drama of World War II. War, not economic wisdom, brought the depression to an end.

Not only is economics without great theater, but when theater is present, economists tend to discount its relevance. This was for long the professional reaction to the crash. It was said to be a response to deeper economic forces. That previous summer there had been a slight, although then largely unnoticed, weakening in economic performance in industrial markets. To this the stock market, with the percipience for which markets are celebrated, was responding, although rather belatedly and violently, to be sure. In the ensuing months autonomous forces inherent in the economy, aggravated perhaps by some bad policy, brought on the depression. The market crash was only an incident.

This is, or was, escapist nonsense. The stock market crash, or more specifically the speculation that made it inevitable, was an economic event of prime importance. Like a blow that shatters glass, its effect was in a deeply vulnerable context; the importance of the blow cannot, for that reason, be dismissed.

In the weeks immediately following October 1929, there was a marked slump in the sales of consumer durables, radios and automobiles being the prominent examples. This was the natural result of would-be purchasers being caught in the market, being associated with those who were or sensing that something was very wrong. The index of industrial production (1928 = 100), which, seasonally adjusted, stood at 111 in October, fell to 106 in November and to 101 in December, the fastest drop since 1920. The leading historian of the depression, Charles P. Kindleberger, takes exception, if cautiously, to the reputable view: 'In the light of the sudden collapse of business, commodity prices, and imports at the end of 1929, it is difficult to maintain that the stock market was a superficial phenomenon, a signal, or a triggering, rather than part of the deflationary mechanism.'[1]

The crash and the causative speculation were, to repeat, not passive reflections of deeper trends in the economy. And,

1. Charles P. Kindleberger, *The World in Depression, 1929–1939*, revised and enlarged edition (Berkeley: University of California Press, 1986), p. 116.

as would the great speculation of the 1980s, they had a solid consequence in the years ahead. The mood of the 1920s that had helped sustain the market and the economy was clearly, irrevocably changed. The way was open for something hitherto unrecognized in economics and reluctantly conceded to this day. That is the possibility of an economic equilibrium with idle plant capacity and persisting unemployment – in short, depression or recession not as an episode but as normal economic performance. This calls for a special word.

In the classical system, as earlier outlined, unused industrial plant and unemployment could not endure. If workers were without work, their services would be offered at a lower price, which would make it worthwhile to employ them. Similarly, if there was unused plant or other productive facility, prices would be lowered to attract customers. Any reluctance in this regard would yield to competition. That would force prices down and sales and production up.

Always there would be a flow of purchasing power sufficient to buy the goods at the prices so established. This was the benign effect of what was known as Say's Law, for J. B. Say (1767–1832), the great French interpreter, organizer and exponent of the highly perceptive but at times somewhat disordered offering of Adam Smith. Say's Law was wonderfully simple: from the sale of any product comes the wherewithal to buy it in the market. In the price, as a matter of utter inevitability, are the wage cost, the interest cost, the rent and the profit (or loss), all together equaling in amount what is necessary to buy it. The flow of income back from the price totals precisely the purchasing power necessary to buy the product. There could, in the nature of the arithmetic, be no shortage of demand. This was revealed truth to conventional economics, and so it was to the reputable world beyond. To question Say's Law was to invite the accusation that one was, if not a crackpot, at least grossly defective in economic training.

It had long been recognized that the economy had waves — good times and less good. There were, as earlier noted, worthy books and university courses on the business cycle. The latter, however, had an autonomous life of its own. Any downswing, however explained, was temporary, a vagrant departure from the full-employment equilibrium.

The sad but inescapable lesson of the 1930s was, as I've said, that there could be continuing unemployment and continuing general depression. The reason is by no means subtle: Say's Law is not immutable. Income does not necessarily get spent or invested; in times of insecurity and doubt as to the future it will be hoarded in cash or in banks, and the banks may be too frightened or pressed by bad loans to lend. Or they may be lacking in suitably solvent borrowers. Also prices do not necessarily accommodate to the reduced demand. In the modern corporate economy they have a certain rigidity or stability, as do wage costs. Accordingly, with reduced demand, production falls and workers are laid off. Their reduced or now-nonexistent income adds to the depressive effect. If personal income is unequally distributed, as it was in that time (and still is), Say's Law may be further defeated by large blocks of unused purchasing power accruing to fortunate individuals who are under no pressure to spend or invest. This is not the case with those of small or moderate income. It is one of the least advertised, and for the very affluent the least attractive, of economic truths that a reasonably equitable distribution of income throughout the society is highly functional.

Eventually, however, as the economy recedes, there is stabilization at a new equilibrium, one with low production and substantial unemployment. Spending by those unaffected or less affected by the slump or those having resources on which they can draw for purchase and consumption does continue. It sustains the economy but at the lower level. And there is no basic reason why this new equilibrium should not be maintained. The belief that there must be an automatic return to high or full utilization of plant and workers depends on political faith, hope and assurance, not on economic reality. The 1930s were a decade-long manifestation of an underemployment equilibrium. It is one of the uses of history that it reminds as to what can happen again.

As the decade of depression passed, there were other factors adding to, sometimes deepening and otherwise sustaining the underemployment equilibrium. By far the most important was the banking crisis – more precisely, the institutional vulnerability of the American banking system. The latter was, as it largely remains, highly decentralized, a reflection in part of a lurking populist suspicion of the power of money and any undue concentration of financial resources in the big money centers, notably in Wall Street. Already before the crash, banks were failing at a rate of roughly two a day and had been for six years.[2] In the next years the number in collapse greatly increased. At the beginning of 1933, runs on

2. Robert L. Heilbroner, *The Worldly Philosophers*, 6th edition (New York: Simon & Schuster, 1986), pp. 251–52.

the banks were of epidemic proportions. In February, Michigan, Maryland and Ohio placed their banks on holiday, and other states soon followed. In March, on becoming President, Franklin Roosevelt extended the bank holiday to the country as a whole. That this unease leading on to panic had a powerfully adverse effect on consumer spending and producer investment none can doubt.

The other factor ensuring the continuation of the depressive equilibrium emerged from the agricultural sector, which, as earlier noted, was still a dominant part of the economy in those years. In the 1920s there had been the juxtaposition of high debt and low prices. Then in the depression years farm prices dropped to hitherto unimagined levels. In the period from 1909 to 1914 the ratio of farm prices to farm costs was given a basic value of 100. This was the famous parity price relationship, which farmers and farm organizations came to regard as having a natural, almost theological origin. 'The farmer is entitled to the parity price.' In 1918, this ratio reached 200; farm prices were twice the parity relationship to costs. In 1929, the parity ratio was down to 138; by 1932, it was a dismal, even murderous 57.[3]

There was also the already mentioned tendency of the agricultural industry (which still persists) to produce more than can be sold at an acceptable price. The large automobile companies, with occasional and aberrant exception, do not produce cars to dump on the market for whatever price they will bring. Agricultural production distributed over thousands and tens of thousands of producers is subject to no such

3. *Yearbook of Agriculture, 1934* (Washington, D.C.: United States Department of Agriculture, 1934), Table 471, p. 706.

restraint. Left to itself, that industry is more than mildly self-destructive as to production and price. One result is that in all agricultural countries almost without exception there is some public mechanism of price and supply management for farm production. To this day this is regarded as politically deviant, a yielding to an everywhere-powerful farm lobby. It is not. One notes again that the industry that most closely conforms to the competitive ideal – to the purest of pure competition – is the least able to tolerate the result and lives, therefore, under the greatest measure of state control of prices and production.

In the United States in the early years of the depression, as in other industrial countries, this control was not imposed immediately. For a time, depressed agricultural prices and incomes, the result of what could only seem an endemic overproduction, added signally to the generally depressed condition – to the persistence and depth of the underemployment equilibrium. In 1929, farm income stood at $9.76 billion in current dollars. By 1933, it had diminished to $4.66 billion. From this, in turn, came a similarly diminished flow of income to those from whom the farmers acquired production needs and the requisites of life.

Nor was this misfortune being suffered quietly. In January 1933, Edward A. O'Neal, head of the Farm Bureau Federation, the most powerful and conservative of the farm organizations (and in later years briefly my employer), told a Senate committee that 'unless something is done for the American farmer we will have revolution in the countryside within less than twelve months.'[4] There is little doubt that

4. Quoted in Arthur M. Schlesinger, Jr., *The Age of Roosevelt*, vol. 2: *The Coming of the New Deal* (Boston: Houghton Mifflin, 1958), p. 27.

this threat was exaggerated, but it admirably expressed the mood of the time.

The problems just cited and that of the depression in general were, from 1931 on, very much a part of my life. There was a considerable personal effect: I graduated from college in the spring of 1931 to no employment opportunity except a graduate fellowship in economics at the University of California at Berkeley, earned by my undergraduate work in the subject and principally by a thesis on farm tenancy in Ontario and its very dismal economic aspects. The fellowship was for the study of agricultural economics. My stipend was partly earned by serving as a research assistant at the then newly created Giannini Foundation of Agricultural Economics. My initial research work was rather specialized; I was assigned to study the production and marketing of California honey. The beekeeping industry was also in poor condition.

In those days discussion of the depression and its causes was part of the daily, almost hourly, routine. Some of my colleagues adhered to the classical orthodoxy. Others questioned whether an economy so obviously adverse in its performance could or should survive. There was relatively little discussion of intermediate efforts at amelioration or repair.

At all times, we heard from Washington assurances that everything would soon be well. They were extraordinarily persistent and, as to content, repetitive. 'The economy is fundamentally sound' or, more succinctly, 'Fundamentals are sound.' (There was to be an echo of the same words as the recession deepened and persisted sixty years later.) Prevalent as well were the predictions of a prompt recovery; they came in a steady flow from Herbert Hoover and the White House. Once he sharply rebuked an appeal for positive action on the depression by saying that the plea was simply too late, the depression had ended some months earlier. He did take one positive step of later resonance: he reduced income taxes. As a stimulating force, however, lowering taxes suffered from the circumstance that they were already verging on insignificance. A taxpayer with an income of $5,000, a very comfortable return in those days, had his or her tax cut by two-thirds. It went from $16.88 to $5.63. Someone with $10,000, roughly the equivalent of $100,000 today, saw his tax go from $120 down to $65.

The tax reduction was, nonetheless, hailed as a bold and constructive step. Again there would be distant echoes; nothing is more constant in depression or recession than the belief that more money for the affluent, not excluding oneself, will work wonders as to recovery. In the event, the depression continued as before.

I did have one early encounter with the prevailing orthodoxy in the concluding days of the 1932 presidential election. Mr. Hoover had carried his campaign to California, and I went with a young colleague to hear him speak at an Oakland railway freight station. It was immediately adjacent to a large field covered with sections of enormous pipe deposited there for a planned but still unbuilt sewer system. Each section had been boarded up at the ends and converted into a residence; the area was one of the more populous of the local Hoovervilles. The occupants were more than adequately available as an audience for the President; they had nothing else to do; they were ready and waiting. Good Republicans coming to hear their leader were, by force of numbers, kept at a considerable distance. Mr. Hoover told of the end of the depression and of the good times already under way. He was greeted with loud, raucous cheers, the nature of which he could not possibly have understood.

By 1932, the index of industrial production stood at 63.4, down from 100 in 1929, the base year. An estimated 12.8 million were unemployed, nearly 25 percent of the labor force. There was still, nonetheless, a solid and influential view that the depression would correct itself, that high or full employment was normal. Present in much economic discussion was emphasis on the need to retain and inspire business confidence. To this end, the role of the government should be limited. A permissible exception was the establishment in December 1931 of the Reconstruction Finance Corporation with the primary purpose of bailing out dangerously vulnerable banks and other financial institutions. Then as now, intervention to support such institutions was acceptable government policy. Unlike welfare support to the poor, it was not thought a burden.

Something was also done in the Hoover years to expedite normal public works expenditures; these were brought to a near record level. The result was a substantial increase in aggregate federal expenditures and the deficit. This, however, was subject to criticism; it was seen as an unfortunate departure from the established canons of conservative public finance. Certainly the government should not deliberately spend money to stimulate the economy; that would be destructive of business confidence and thus, quite possibly, would make the depression worse.

In the election campaign of 1932, Roosevelt was not greatly in disagreement. He too promised fiscal responsibility, strong steps toward a balanced budget. Later, in 1936, when he asked Samuel Rosenman, his highly accomplished assistant, how he might reconcile the spending and deficits of his first four years with the promise of strict fiscal rectitude that he had made in a speech in Pittsburgh in 1932, he was told, according to legend, that his only course was to deny firmly that he had ever given that speech.

In the months between his election and his inauguration, Roosevelt was asked by Herbert Hoover to help restore business confidence by a strong affirmation of economic conservatism. Addressing his successor in February 1933, Mr. Hoover suggested that they join in the responsible guiding view:

> It would steady the country greatly if there could be prompt assurance that there will be no tampering or inflation of the currency; that the budget will be unquestionably balanced, even if further taxation is necessary; that the Government credit will be maintained by refusal to exhaust it in the issue of securities.[5]

Roosevelt did not respond as requested, but nothing in his campaign had expressed a noticeably different intention.

There is a larger point here: no more than would President George Bush sixty years later did President Hoover like a depression or recession. But both had a constituency among whom a large number personally preferred depressed econ-

---

5. Quoted in Arthur M. Schlesinger, Jr., *The Age of Roosevelt*, vol. 1: *The Crisis of the Old Order* (Boston: Houghton Mifflin, 1957), p. 476.

---

omic conditions to the countering action. Unemployment did not affect them in any personal way. Perhaps it eased labor relations and made the workers they employed more concerned with their jobs, more amenable to factor and employer discipline. Others in secure professional or financial positions could also view the economic scene with personal detachment. For many, and especially for many with political voice, money and influence, depression or recession is far from painful. This no one can openly avow; on some things one must be discreet, even in self-revelation.

The depression spread from the United States to the industrialized countries around the world. In Britain it added force to the already depressed conditions following upon the overvaluation of sterling. In Germany it increased the pressure on the continuing fragile political structure of the Weimar Republic. In the early depression years Germany was still being asked for reparations (as I've told earlier, they were finally ended by Hitler in 1933) and was suffering from the peculiarly disastrous internal policies of Chancellor Brüning. These included direct downward pressure on wages, interest and the prices of cartelized industries; on December 8, 1931, all wages were rolled back to the level prevailing on January 10, 1927. There was a rigorous refusal to allow any increased public works expenditure or like support to the economy. In the winter of 1931–32, unemployment in Germany stood at more than 40 percent of the labor force. An incisive contemporary observer said that Brüning's 'suicidal policy stemmed from his general philosophy. He feared the phantom of a runaway inflation; he did not like the idea of pampering the unemployed by creating jobs.'[6] Inexorably the way was thus paved for Adolf Hitler.

The depression also led to action by the central banks of the industrial countries, including the Federal Reserve. (On this I will have a later word.) And it led to steps to protect domestic industry and employment by curtailing imports. Here the United States took a leading role. Already in June 1930, and over the strongly expressed opposition of a full thousand economists, the Congress had passed the Smoot-Hawley tariff bill protecting a wide range of industrial products and with a special orientation to agriculture.

Over the rest of the industrial world there was a broad response: Italy, France, Canada, Cuba, Mexico, Australia and New Zealand all took similar or retaliatory action. Even the Swiss were moved to seek limitations on American imports in response to an increased tariff on Swiss watches. There is always pleasure in seeing wide agreement on a specific course of action among governments that are seeking solutions to some common problem. That is not so when, as happened in this case, the result was to make everyone's position worse.

6. W. S. Woytinsky, *Stormy Passage: A Personal History Through Two Russian Revolutions to Democracy and Freedom: 1905–1960* (New York: Vanguard Press, 1961), p. 466.

9

The New Deal

This account has until now derived from the efforts of a young scholar to learn of the economic world as it was in his youth and of what had gone immediately before. It has combined some personal observation with the yield from rather more serious later study. Beginning in 1934, however, I became associated with the economic programs of the New Deal. In the spring of that year I went to work for the Agricultural Adjustment Administration – the Triple A – with the title of Associate Economist. I was assigned to study the feasibility of having the federal government take over the tax-delinquent and reverted lands of local governments and enter them in a new public domain. The latter would have been vast. I so urged but to no avail. In later times I frequently traveled to Washington on one assignment or another from my new teaching post at Harvard. I had become, in greater or lesser measure, a participant in national economic affairs. So there is here a modest change in my narrative. No doubt there is also a danger in telling of participation; one is strongly tempted to attribute primary importance to that in which one has had a part.

When I arrived in Washington in the first full year of the Roosevelt administration, my dominant impression was of a wonderful excitement, a deep commitment to action and a considerable uncertainty as to what should be done. The uncertainty added to the excitement; it meant that almost anyone could speak and sometimes even be heard on the needed course. It was a further advantage that so many of us were so young. I speak here of the hundreds who were brought or attracted to the capital for the new tasks and by the needed employment of the New Deal. No one was silenced on grounds that he (women were rare in our ranks) lacked age and experience; having either was a claim few could make.

One small but highly articulate and even somewhat disciplined group there, as earlier at Berkeley, did unite on the need to abolish the system entirely – to accept that capitalism was a failure. Communism was the obvious alternative, the Communist Party the obvious instrument. In later times the role of those so committed in the New Deal years has been both minimized and greatly exaggerated. In fact, the youthful Communists and their associates were a small, if vocal, part of the New Deal community. They attracted an audience and prestige because of the exuberant assurance with which they held to and stated their views. Had such views not been present among those descending on Washington, it would have been surprising. No one of any sensitivity could look on capitalism in those years and think it a success. There was, accordingly, a choice between repair and revolt. As the previous chapter has told, even responsible and broadly conservative leaders, including those of the farm lobby, spoke openly of the possibility of revolt.

Those seeking repair, either from choice, instinct or the desire for a measure of political acceptability, were the clearly dominant influence, and with them I was allied. In the absence of any overall design, their answer – our answer – was a kind of activist pragmatism. One urged what seemed to serve the particular case. Most such action was, in one degree or another, in conflict with the established economic orthodoxy. We were at odds with the no longer quite believable benignity of the market or, where public expenditure was concerned, the canons of sound finance and the balanced budget. Or, on monetary matters, with the all but sacrosanct gold standard. In the mood of Washington at the time there was a marked pleasure in questioning the established view and in the outrage so provoked.

The sharpest collision between the orthodox prescription and the seemingly pragmatic course was the NRA – the National Recovery Act. This legislation, nearly all solemn history to the contrary, was rather plausible. Over the heartland of the industrial economy, firms were having to cut their prices because of the general contraction of demand. Being so compelled, they, in turn, cut wages and laid off workers. The price reductions brought the wage reductions and unemployment, and these, in turn, limited the flow of aggregate demand and intensified the depression.

The remedy seemed obvious. Allow the firms in each industry to come together to restrain price cutting and therewith wage reduction and the consequent unemployment. This was the essence of the industry code, which was the centerpiece of the policy. Then, as a concession to the labor force, let workers come together in unions – the celebrated

Section 7A of the National Recovery Act — to protect and affirm their collective interest. And let all this be celebrated in a gala exercise with publicity and parades; let the Blue Eagle, symbol of the effort, be everywhere ascendant to improve business and public morale. Nothing, then as now, was more emphasized by the business community than the importance of its own morale.

However plausible, it would be hard to imagine a policy in more abrasive conflict with conventional economic theory. Gone was the competitive market; gone was competition, in common reference free competition, the very linchpin of the classical system. It had been, as I have told, the essence of the liberal theology from the nineteenth century on that the public good was always served by more competition, never by less. It was this that the antitrust laws, preeminently a liberal prescription, were designed to ensure. Within the New Deal community, a large, even dominant, group saw monopoly and imperfect competition and its restriction on output as a basic cause of the underemployment equilibrium. This was, broadly, the thesis of my first book, *Modern Competition and Business Policy*,[1] written with the noted liberal industrialist Henry S. Dennison. Its publication coincided almost precisely with my emerging doubts as to the validity of its argument, and in ensuing years I thoughtfully omitted it from my list of published writings.

The decision of the Supreme Court on May 27, 1935, in the Schecter Poultry Corporation case, to delete the NRA was not greatly regretted, even by the New Deal economic com-

1. New York: Oxford University Press, 1938.

munity. To this day, few economists or historians have spoken in its favor.

Although in Germany and Japan the industrial cartel has long been seen as consistent with economic well-being and economic growth, that is not the case in the United States. Perhaps the powerfully stimulated price and wage reductions in those years were, indeed, a depressive force. The NRA may well have been a more pragmatic accommodation to the current condition than was then or since supposed. *Requiescat* nonetheless.

The farm program also involved a sharp conflict with the orthodox view. The agricultural industry, as I have sufficiently noted, was characterized by the classic competitive structure: many producers selling completely undifferentiated products under conditions of perfect competition. The buyers of those products – grain merchants, cotton merchants, canners, packers, processors, tobacco firms – were not equally so numerous and not so perfectly competitive. Yet this was hardly the case for a policy reducing and controlling agricultural output. Low prices, in the classical view, had their own implicit remedy; they curtailed production, and prices then stabilized or improved. A huge government-sponsored agricultural cartel was surely not the answer; certainly it could not be reconciled with free-market orthodoxy.

On the whole, however, the control of production and prices in the agricultural sector brought less opposition than did the NRA. That was because agriculture, as is still the case today, exists outside the main current of economic thought. It was particularly important in 1933 (as later) that it had its own specialized economics and economists – agricultural economics and agricultural economists standing apart. It was the agricultural economists, under the approving ministry of Secretary of Agriculture Henry Agard Wallace, who designed and directed the farm program. Those of us who participated were regarded by the larger economic world as the slightly eccentric exponents of a special case.

The Supreme Court, then the stalwart defender of orthodox attitudes, outlawed much of the original agricultural legislation on the grounds of misuse of the taxing power and invasion of states' rights. However, replacement legislation was quickly devised, and price guarantees and production controls continued, as they do to this day.

The third New Deal innovation involved money. Few matters have been more studied with less clarity of result than the role of monetary policy in the years of the depression. This policy had an orthodox and a highly unorthodox expression, both of which had one thing in common: they seemed bright as to prospect but were deeply disappointing as to result.

The orthodox course of monetary policy called for lower interest rates by the Federal Reserve System and, as then and later denoted, open-market operations. The latter, involving the purchase of government securities by the Federal Reserve, were designed to supply the commercial banks with ample or more than ample loanable funds. These they would then have available for a hoped-for army of eager borrowers who would be attracted by both the availability of the money and the low interest rates.

This policy went back to the Hoover years. Central banks and money have their own magic, and for conservatives even more than for liberals. Interest rates were, indeed, brought down under the New Deal; banks accumulated reserves of such loanable funds in wondrous amounts. The volume of excess reserves – bank funds in excess of reserve requirements – eventually became a commonly cited statistic of the day.[2] Alas, however, the borrowers did not come or, if they did, the banks saw their prospects, given the controlling economic conditions, as unduly and unsafely dim. Not for the first time and certainly not for the last, Federal Reserve policy for expanding the economy was a grave disappointment. You can pull but not push on a string.

There was another, more exotic and unorthodox course of action. That was the Roosevelt gold-buying program of 1933, one of the more spectacular exercises in the checkered history of monetary policy.

The origins of this plan were also, oddly enough, in agriculture: two Cornell University agricultural economists, George F. Warren and Frank A. Pearson, had observed and outlined a century-old association between the price of gold and the level of prices, including, in particular, the prices of farm products, the decisive factor in the farm depression. The association was not surprising. Gold prices had an obvious tendency to rise during periods of price inflation, as, for example, during the Civil War, when people sought refuge in hard, reliable money. In times of depressed prices the value of gold was stable or subsiding; people no longer sought it as a refuge. The two scholars saw an opportunity here. Bid up the price of gold, and other prices would go higher, as in the past. Roosevelt and some around him were persuaded. It was

2. Kindleberger, *The World in Depression*, p. 185.

an especially attractive policy for the farm belt, where prices, which farmers had linked since the days of William Jennings Bryan to the crucifying role of gold, were very bad.

In October 1933, after earlier requiring that all private gold holdings be turned in to the government – the windfall would otherwise have been too wonderful – the President, Secretary of the Treasury Henry Morgenthau and Jesse Jones, the head of the Reconstruction Finance Corporation, which was the purchasing agent, met each morning to set a new and higher price for newly mined gold. Later the sale of foreign gold holdings was invited. The dollar depreciated on the foreign exchanges and would have done so further had not Britain and France been following policies with similar effect. Britain, in particular, had by now abandoned the fixed parity of the pound with the dollar and gold that Keynes had so eloquently condemned and which, internally, had wrought such social havoc.

The gold purchases continued. There was some benefit for export products; overall, the result was deeply disappointing. In the closing weeks of 1933, the price indices went down still more. The gold-buying policy was brought to an end, and on February 1, 1934, gold was stabilized at thirty-five dollars an ounce, a price at which it remained for the next many years.

It is entirely possible that without the gold purchases, the higher gold prices and the depreciating or stabilizing effect on the dollar on foreign exchanges, domestic prices, particularly those for farm exports, might have been worse. We would have stood alone while other countries let their currencies fall and their exports cheapen, thus making their American imports greatly more expensive. This was rarely mentioned at the time and has been little mentioned since.

In its day the gold-buying experiment was the most criticized of all the New Deal policies, and it had the fewest defenders, indeed almost none at all. The more prominent of the New Dealers either privately criticized or detached themselves. Two high officials of the Treasury, Dean Acheson and James Warburg, the distinguished son of Paul M. Warburg, resigned in protest, although Warburg, a stalwart liberal, later regretted his decision. Forty economists gathered under the leadership of E. W. Kemmerer of Princeton University, the most distinguished monetary authority of the 1930s, to form the Economists' National Committee on Monetary Policy. Its purpose, its only purpose, was to fight the gold-purchase insanity. From the New York financial community came an even stronger condemnation: in the most serious depression and most painful price deflation in modern history there were urgent warnings of the imminent danger of inflation. Again the financially encased mind.

As a young scholar viewing the gold-buying program and, indeed, lecturing on it in 1933–34 in my first teaching post at the University of California, I was caught up in a difficult conflict. On the one hand, there was the weight of the respectable position, which I then shared. On the other, there was my all but automatic support of F.D.R. I eventually resolved the matter by dismissing the whole gold-buying episode from mind. This, in large measure, has been its historical fate.

There remained the fourth and by far the most essential pillar of the New Deal policy: the direct employment of the unemployed by the deliberate creation of jobs. This was done through the PWA, or Public Works Administration, and the WPA, or Works Progress Administration. The PWA had its justification in the things it built: office buildings, bridges and other public structures. The WPA had its justification in the jobs it created. Its prime measure of success was not what was done but the number of those employed in doing it. This fact, predictably, was seized upon by conservatives – reference to make-work and to leaf raking became part of the language of the time. In fact, in a wide variety of fields extending on to the theater and the arts, extraordinarily useful work was done.

That these programs were central to the New Deal was made evident by their leadership. Harold L. Ickes, in charge of the PWA, and Harry Hopkins, in charge of the WPA, were the chief Roosevelt lieutenants. To those of us who were young and new to Washington they, along with Secretary Henry A. Wallace, embodied the living heart of the Roosevelt program.

Employment, to repeat, was the principal focus of this effort and for a wholly simple reason: the dominant feature of the underemployment equilibrium is unemployment. The unequivocal need, here dependent on no intervening theory, is to create employment.[3]

It was around these two programs – the PWA and the WPA – that most New Deal thinking turned. They were its solid

---

3. As I will later tell (see p. 110), I headed a major study of these programs in the latter 1930s for the National Resources Planning Board, which resulted in the publication of *The Economic Effects of the Federal Public Works Expenditures, 1933–1938* (Washington, D.C.: National Resources Planning Board, United States Government Printing Office, November 1940).

substance. But here once more was the same problem: an obvious and mortal conflict with traditional, established economic doctrine and practice. Both doctrine and practice emphasized, even assumed, fiscal responsibility, meaning that government must have revenues to cover its expenditures. Under stress of war some departure could be allowed, much as it might even then be regretted. In peacetime, this was unthinkable. And to raise taxes in a depression to cover job-creating expenditure was obviously out of the question; a deeper instinct told that this might be deflationary.

The employment programs required money; that was arithmetically obvious. The accepted orthodoxy, including Roosevelt's own preelection promises, denied the money. How reconcile the obvious remedy for unemployment with the stern denial of what was obviously essential?

To those of us observing or involved, the problem seemed inescapable. Two realities were clashing. Perhaps one should look elsewhere for fault and remedy — perhaps, as earlier noted, to monopoly and its control of supply. But the NRA excluded that. There must somewhere be an answer. Sternly evident was the fact that job creation must be with borrowed money, but to borrow money was totally at odds with the accepted orthodoxy.

Or was it? In the mid-1930s, the problem was wonderfully solved when the most influential voice in economics of the century came to the rescue. His resolution of the conflict between fiscal orthodoxy and economic necessity endures to this day, and not least in recent conservative fiscal practice. To this, the world of John Maynard Keynes, I turn in the next chapter. But first there must be mention of another, different and vitally important New Deal initiative: Social Security.

The Social Security Act, passed in 1935, provided, although at distinctly modest, even primitive levels, old age pensions and unemployment compensation. The bill was drafted by a young lawyer, Thomas H. Eliot, whose delightful account of its legislative and political history can be found in *Recollections of the New Deal: When the People Mattered*,[4] published just after his death in 1991. In the broad sweep of world economic events, the American Social Security legislation was not a highly innovative step. The need for protection of the old and the unemployed is inescapably allied with industrial development and had for long been so recognized. An agricultural society has its own inbuilt system of social security. The farms or peasant holdings pass on to offspring, and the latter, often by rigorously enforced custom, look after their elders. A major reason for rural population increase in much of the world is the need to be assured of sons who will do the work in the fields and be responsible for their parents in their old age. As to unemployment compensation, there is the stolid fact that there is no real unemployment on a farm. By lowering the effective wage, some or much of which may be earned in kind, some employment can always be provided or invented.

It is with industry and urbanization that both old age pensions and unemployment compensation become socially essential. It is then that, with a much-loosened family struc-

---

4. Boston: Northeastern University Press, 1992. It was my privilege to edit the volume and write the introduction.

ture, the old have no support, the unemployed have no income.

To these harsh, inescapable facts of modern life the older industrial countries had long made accommodation – as noted, in Germany under Bismarck in the 1880s, in Britain under Lloyd George in the first decades of the twentieth century, in other European countries at various times. It was a step marked in each case by controversy and objection. In Britain the passage, including through the House of Lords, of legislation providing social security provoked a major constitutional crisis. The opposition in the United States was also adequately bitter.

One conservative member of the Congress not given to understatement said, 'Never in the history of the world has any measure been brought in here so insidiously designed as to prevent business recovery, to enslave workers, and to prevent any possibility of the employers providing work for the people.' Another, succinct but even more dramatic, said, 'The lash of the dictator will be felt.' An Ohio Chamber of Commerce official of strong historical bent found that similar measures had brought the fall of Rome.[5]

In truth, it would be hard to identify any measure that has done more to help secure the future of capitalism. On the one hand, Social Security mitigates the two most aggressive cruelties of the industrial system – impoverishment because of unemployment, impoverishment because of age – and thus calms the associated anger. And, on the other hand, it contributes a reliable flow of income and aggregate demand

5. See Schlesinger, *The Coming of the New Deal*, p. 311. I have cited these and other objections in *Economics in Perspective* (Boston: Houghton Mifflin, 1987), pp. 217–18.

or purchasing power that is wholly recession-proof and that, indeed, rises in less good times to make the economy at least marginally more secure.

None of this was persuasive to the opposition. Those who enjoy good fortune in the economic system, as ever and as now, attribute virtue to themselves and to the system as it stands. All change is thus to be resisted. No plea of personal well-being and possible personal cost can be entered; that would be too crude. Instead it is said that the larger integrity of the system and its functioning must be protected and furthered. Some things do not change. The comfortable, we shall see, similarly so contend some sixty years later.

Social Security succeeded; the requisite legislation, as I have noted, was passed in 1935. It preceded by a year the greatest worldwide invasion of orthodox economic thought of the time, indeed of the century. Neither economic policy nor economics as it is taught would ever again be quite the same. None who saw and experienced this change ever forgot the glow. We were indeed present at the creation.

10

Revolution by John Maynard Keynes

There was much beyond public works and work relief for which the New Deal needed money. Other emergency programs – the Federal Emergency Relief Administration for direct relief of the impoverished, which had been partly inherited from President Hoover; the farm programs; the Tennessee Valley Authority; Rural Electrification and the especially relevant Civilian Conservation Corps, which took young men off the streets and into the forests (Camp David, the presidential retreat in the Maryland hills, is a former CCC camp) – all required cash. They all added to the regular national expenditures, and government revenues for normal governmental functions in the 1930s reflected the current dismal state of the economy. Federal expenditures in 1929 were $3.1 billion in current dollars from revenues of $3.9 billion. By 1933, expenditures were $4.6 billion, revenues $1.99 billion.

The conflict here with the canons of orthodox finance has been sufficiently stressed. Concern extended deeply into the economics profession and to the New Dealers themselves. None, or at least not many, could allow themselves to believe or certainly to say that these deficits were tolerable. None could find utility, much less merit, therein.

As the depression strengthened and the faith in the self-correcting tendency of the business cycle weakened, there was a search for economic flaw and remedial action. The possible role of monopoly or more general imperfection in the market economy I have already mentioned. That recovery might come from increased public spending, an increased public deficit, was well beyond the range of responsible thought. A deficit reflected, at best, harsh necessity. Certainly it had no positive value. Or so it was until what came to be called the Age of Keynes.

In 1933, the voice of John Maynard Keynes was already one to be reckoned with. His response to the Treaty of Versailles has been noted, as also his stunning attack on Winston Churchill and the by-now-acknowledged error in the British return to gold in 1925. He had criticized the high churchmen of the covenanted political and financial religion, and he had been shown to be right. Now he took on the whole world of economics on its most compelling, even sacred belief. He said that the deficit had economic virtue, that it should be larger. To increase it was the path, indeed the only path, to recovery. The shock to conventional attitudes can hardly be exaggerated.

In the rather tightly disciplined government at Westminster he was regarded as indubitably brilliant but nonetheless inconvenient and perhaps even eccentric. Not a person wholly to be trusted. His primary thrust, accordingly, was directed at, as he saw it, the economically decisive and possibly more open-minded American polity and policy. This occurred on December 31, 1933, the last day of the tenth month of the New Deal. It was in an Open Letter to President Roosevelt, which, not exactly as an afterthought, he published in the *New York Times*. The message was simple; it stressed his belief that the administration in Washington should place 'overwhelming emphasis on the increase of national purchasing power resulting from governmental expenditure which is financed by loans.'[1]

The letter and his subsequent visits to F.D.R. have been far from overlooked in the history of the New Deal. At the time, in fact, they had little effect. The established view was little influenced by a mere letter. The decisive influence was to come two years later. Not since Adam Smith and Karl Marx would ideas, the role of which Keynes was not himself disposed to minimize, have such an effect on public attitude and action.

The ideas were twofold. They were set forth in his *General Theory of Employment Interest and Money*. This was a complex, ill-organized, often obscure book, which owed much of its influence to the intermediary role of economists, mostly younger members of the profession, who read it and conveyed the central themes to a larger public and to the relevant political world.

The book's first and fundamental point, already emphasized, was that the depression was by nature no temporary thing, no self-correcting manifestation of the business cycle. Nor was it a brief departure from the normal or full-employment equilibrium. Keynes held that, as the enduring depression was making sadly plausible, the economy could

1. Keynes, 'Open Letter,' *New York Times*, December 31, 1933.

find its equilibrium with unemployment and underutilized plant capacity. Some of the income flowing back from the wages, interest, rents and profits that comprise the sales price of a product might, indeed, not be spent or invested.

In the depression context there could, in Keynes's words, be a liquidity preference – a strong desire to sit on the cash as it came in or keep its unspent, unloaned equivalent in a bank. Production would then spiral down and stay at the level where need forced the requisite consumer (and investment) spending.

Cutting wages – the traditional way to sustain employment – might now, instead, add to unemployment. In the classical design, it was thought profitable to add workers as the wage went down; production would be greater, and more could be sold at the lower cost and price. Now the plausible effect of wage reduction was to lower worker income and spending, and have lessened demand, smaller sales, more unemployment. Attention had to be paid to what would soon become a commonplace concern: the effect of any economic development or public action on the larger flow of purchasing power – on, as it would be called, aggregate demand. Economics had always occupied itself with the microeconomics of the market – the adjustment of wages and costs to prices, and the reverse. Here entered macroeconomics, the general flow of purchasing power in the system as a whole.

The second of the Keynesian contributions derived immutably from the first: to break the underemployment equilibrium and increase output and employment, you must supplement aggregate demand or purchasing power. The only sure way of doing this is to have the government borrow the unspent funds or, more precisely, their equivalent and by spending them add to aggregate demand and employment. Such was the formidable justification for what harsh circumstance had already, in some measure, required.

The economists who adopted, interpreted and applied the Keynesian view were, with the help of the controlling circumstance, the most influential of their generation. From the University of Cambridge and Cambridge, England, the word came to Harvard University and Cambridge, Massachusetts. And it was in substantial measure from there that it went on to Washington, D.C. Not often has a university been so actively involved in a revolution.[2]

One must, as ever, be careful in citing one's role in history; there is nothing critics are more keen to correct. I was, however, a fairly visible member of the Harvard Keynesian community. After reading *The General Theory* in 1936, I went the following year to Cambridge, England, intending to have several terms of firsthand study with the master. It was the time of Keynes's first heart attack; he did not appear at the university that academic year. Among his younger acolytes – R. F. Kahn, later Lord Kahn; Joan Robinson, who was to be my lifelong friend; Piero Sraffa, the brilliant Italian economist, resident in Trinity College; and the superbly innovative Polish economist, Michal Kalecki – the discussion of the Keynesian thesis and its political meaning, one in which I joined, continued by day and by night. It did not add greatly to the central ideas; it did deeply confirm the now-revealed truth.

I went also to Germany and to Sweden to study the parallel

2. See John Kenneth Galbraith, 'How Keynes Came to America,' in *Economics, Peace and Laughter* (Boston: Houghton Mifflin, 1971), pp. 43–59.

manifestations of Keynesian policy there. On this there will
be later comment.

I returned to Harvard in the autumn of 1938 to find the
discussion of Keynesian policy even more intense at home.
Much of it was under the aegis of Professor Alvin Harvey
Hansen, who, at first a critic of Keynes, had become his
strongest American voice. More than a Harvard audience was
now involved: responsible officials came from Washington to
participate in Hansen's seminars, and the nightly train carried
my academic colleagues to Washington to advise and consult
with sympathetic or merely accessible officials there. In 1939,
as earlier told, I spent much time in Washington myself,
directing a major retrospective study of the public-works and
public-employment experience. Not surprisingly, though not
without controversy (it was, indeed, sharp), my report gave a
full and unduly optimistic endorsement to the Keynesian
interpretation of this experience. 'The view that depressions
will correct themselves if left alone is by no means dead, but
there is grave doubt if it is likely to become again the basis of
public policy.'[3]

Prior to the appearance of *The General Theory*, there had been
some movement in this direction. Marriner Eccles, the Chairman of the Federal Reserve Board, and Lauchlin Currie, its
most influential staff member, had been thinking and, on
occasion, speaking in similar terms. Accepting the all too
evident limits of monetary policy – cheap loanable funds that

3. Galbraith, *The Economic Effects of the Federal Public Works Expenditures,
1933–1938*, p. 4.

no one borrowed – they had urged as necessary direct fiscal stimulus and government support to purchasing power. They were heard but were thought mildly eccentric; these were bizarre ideas to emerge from, of all places, a central bank! Now, with the high authority of Keynes, there was a union of Keynesians and those who, under the pressure of experience, had come to accept the practical policy. Moving to the White House as the first economic adviser to a President, Currie used his office and prestige to bring people of reliable Keynesian view to positions of economic importance in the various government departments. It was thus that I later became involved in price control operations.

To the extent that a Marxist cabal existed in the New Deal, it was, as I've said, of slight significance. A Keynesian consortium *was* a reality: there was an informal but close association of those known to accept and urge the Keynesian view. Had the influence of this consortium been fully appreciated, it would have been thought not less dangerous than that of Karl Marx. And as the Keynesian ideas gained recognition and a following, so, indeed, did the orthodox paranoia. Keynesians were dangerous people; scholars of decent respectability and appropriate caution kept clear.

As Roosevelt's first term passed, the economy improved – slowly. Farm prices and income recovered somewhat; so did industrial activity in general. By 1936, national product, the aggregate of all productive activity, was back at 1929 levels, although the economic performance was remarkably uneven. The economic measures of the New Deal were having an effect; so, in an agreeably unplanned way, was an action that had preceded the major Keynesian discussion. That was the payment in government bonds of the previously authorized bonus of nearly $2 billion to veterans of the First World War.

This payment was passed by the Congress in 1936 over a presidential veto. President Roosevelt, still hearing clearly the voice of conservative finance, appealed to the veterans after the passage of the act not to cash and spend from their reward; it was advice that, fortunately, a singularly small number followed.

In succeeding months the notion that a boom – unemployment and other depressive factors notwithstanding – might be getting out of hand went to the highest levels of the government. There was a strong movement to retrench. In calendar year 1937, the deficit was greatly reduced, and the economy took another plunge. This was the first recession, so called, in history; in its original definition it was an unfortunate adverse economic movement while the economy was emerging from a depression. Given the history – recovery with strong government support to the economy, then a sharp downturn with curtailment of that support – one could scarcely imagine a more compelling affirmation of the Keynesian design. And there was more to come.

The underemployment equilibrium would be broken decisively with the coming of the war and the consequent and massive government expenditure. In later years a Republican President, Richard Nixon, would proclaim that 'we are all Keynesians now,' and another, Ronald Reagan, though amiably innocent of its source, would carry to damaging extremes the Keynesian acceptance of government fiscal support to the economy. It was in the 1930s that it all began. Not often in history do ideas and events combine so decisively to persuade.

*

The Keynesian system also provided an essential counterpart to the remedies for depression: a policy for good times. Then, when tax revenues were rising and social needs were diminishing, the deficit should be reduced. There was one fiscal remedy for depression, its opposite when the economy was strong.

This need for a reversal of course would eventually be the dark side of Keynesian fiscal policy or macroeconomic policy, as it would henceforth be called. For, as resistant as orthodox opinion might be to deficits, that resistance was slight as compared with the political problems posed by trying to reduce them in good times. Both the needed increase in taxes and the needed reduction in expenditures would be powerfully and sometimes bitterly opposed. The point should be made more frequently: Keynes was a far better prophet for recession and depression than for prosperity and associated and often banal optimism. In both depression and prosperity, the singular feature of Keynesian fiscal policy would be the political power and mental rigidity of the forces with which it had to contend.

John Maynard Keynes was, all would agree, quintessentially English. Yet, as has been observed and as he was later to say, he found his strongest support and the greatest number of followers in the United States. It was here that the Keynesian history was made. The 1930s were, however, seminal years in other countries as well – in Sweden, Canada, Britain, Germany and Japan and elsewhere. In all except Japan it was my good fortune to be present and to observe.

11

The Larger World

In June of 1933, three months and a few days after Roosevelt's inauguration, leaders (or their most distinguished representatives) of the major industrial countries of the time, along with quite a few others, assembled in London to consider what by way of joint or agreed action could be done to mitigate what was now clearly a world crisis.

The conference that followed was an occasion of extraordinary confusion. For a generation and more thereafter, economists and economic historians would seek to make sense of what had been intended, advocated or merely said. An idle quest. In fact, there were only two real issues, both obvious and banal.

Since the onset of the depression, governments had sought to encourage their exports and discourage imports by abandoning the gold standard and allowing their currencies to depreciate on the international exchanges. Their plan was to make exports cheap and imported goods more expensive in order to provide a generalized form of protection, but, needless to say, this invited countervailing action by other countries. The British had abandoned the old gold content and dollar parity of the pound that Keynes had criticized, and the United States was about to initiate the gold-purchase program. In one way or another, other countries were similarly depreciating their currencies to improve their economic position, which resulted in counterpart damage elsewhere.

The second concern was forthright tariff protection. Countries that were in the midst of depression had taken steps to protect their domestic industries and employment by imposing or raising tariffs. The United States had done this through the earlier-mentioned Smoot-Hawley legislation, and, by 1932, abandoning a near century of commitment to free trade, the British had put a tariff ring around what was still, in all ordinary reference, the British Empire.

The purpose of the London Economic Conference, as it was called, was, in the largest sense, to decide whether countries would go it alone on tariffs, currency depreciation and economic policy in general or join in a common commitment to currency stabilization and tariff restraint, in some measure placing themselves at the mercy of the vagrant winds of world markets.

It was Roosevelt and the United States that decided matters. Nations, and specifically the United States, would take charge of their own future; they would not be inhibited by international understandings or agreements. 'The sound internal economic system of a nation is a greater factor in its well being than the price of its currency.' There should be no concessions to the 'old fetishes of so-called international bankers.'[1] That was the message of President Roosevelt to the

---

1. United States Department of State, *Foreign Relations of the United States, Diplomatic Papers*, vol. 1 (1933), p. 673.

Conference, and it may well have been the clearest statement of policy ever made by a major head of state on such an occasion. It was not necessarily his best; it brought the Conference to an end, and, in practical effect, before it had begun.

Modern industrial capitalism, as will later be seen, is essentially an international system, but the 1930s were to witness a return to the older, more violent nationalism. A pattern of policy was established or perhaps, more precisely, affirmed which was to be followed by the United States but even more strongly by the entire world. It was not international but autarchical in mood. What would count was not what could be done as an exercise in joint responsibility; it was what each country could do for itself.

Traveling through Europe, as later I did in 1937 and 1938 – France, Germany, Italy, Austria, Czechoslovakia, Poland, Scandinavia – one passed through a maze of currency restrictions, customs inspections and tourist concessions in the form of cheap money and gasoline, all a small indication of what was being encountered in larger international trade. Nor were these measures at their most damaging in purely economic terms. It was the political extremism, the intense and even insane nationalism so cultivated, that would set the stage for the descent into military conflict in the years to come.

By 1932, the British economy was showing some signs of recovery. Employment and industrial output were back, more or less, to the 1929 level. Domestic investment, especially in housing, had increased. Here, perhaps, monetary policy had some positive effect. The Bank of England reduced its lending rate to a distinctly modest 2 percent, and public and private lending rates came down to near-nominal levels. There was also a small increase in public expenditure, though no deliberate effort thus to stimulate production and employment.

Even with the protective steps that were taken, Britain was still, relatively speaking, an open trading economy. This meant that some, perhaps quite a bit, of any fiscal stimulation would be lost to foreigners because of increased purchases of imported products. In any case, the government was not noticeably receptive to such action. As told, the voice of Lord Keynes was heard far less clearly in Westminster than in Washington.

While, however, the 1929 level was regained, that was the low point of the 1920s. The improvement was only to the level of previous depression. For the rest of the 1930s the British economic performance was far from brilliant; for many workers the dole remained a way of life. Unemployment declined only slowly, from 17.6 percent in 1932 to between 12 and 13 percent in 1935. For anyone living in Britain in those years (or later), and certainly for a student of economics as was I, the depression was still the urgent issue. All economics was reduced to a discussion of its cause and cure. As in the United States, recovery in Britain would await the real lift that would be given by arms expenditure, mobilization and war.

Of all the larger European countries, France was the least affected by the depression, and it was thus the most moderate in its response. The reason lies deep in French social character and polity and is insufficiently recognized to this day.

In most countries, and particularly in the United States, economics and the economy are central to life and, needless to say, to government and politics. In France, all but uniquely, this is not so. There economics is secondary to social and cultural concerns, and especially as these impinge on affairs of state. Excitement over economic policy is muted. In its lesser role, the economic life of France was an inherent stability that is not the good fortune of any other major country. There is opportunity for simple, obvious corrective action and for a controlling pragmatism.

More evident, perhaps, is the calm French response to the economic prospect and change. The speculative mood that is endemic in the United States, Britain and Japan is more rarely present in France. No part of Paris is identified, as are Wall Street and the City, with finance, high finance and recurrent excess. In 1719, John Law had brought a fever of speculation to Rue Quincampoix and later to the Place Vendôme, where, it is recorded, women came to exchange their virtue for stock in the Mississippi Company, the custodian of vast gold reserves in Louisiana which, to this day, remain undiscovered. The French learned well the lesson of history; ever since 1719, financial euphoria has been for other countries. For all these reasons the French were spared the 1929 disaster.

In the later depression years, governments rose and fell in France, the franc was eventually and reluctantly devalued, there were various decrees affecting wages and employment – it was generally thought well to raise wages to support purchasing power – and government construction and eventual rearmament gave a measure of support to the economy. These were not precisely happy times in France; nonetheless, no other major country found the depression so mildly oppressive. Not committed to any clear-cut policy and with an economy of inherent stability, the French survived much better than their neighbors.

Germany, on the other hand, was the most distraught economic case in the early depression years; it was also the clearest case of action by the state to promote economic recovery. That this was accomplished under a government of repression, genocide and eventual military insanity has, in some measure, kept the economic achievement from being seen. Nothing constructive could be thought to come from Adolf Hitler. In reality, the German economy made a remarkable recovery in the depression years – the depression there was effectively over by 1936 – and this fact remains to this day largely outside the common reach of history.

In 1933, when, a few weeks before Roosevelt, Hitler came to power, the German economic condition was impressively bad. The Brüning policy had been, as already told, one of recovery through hardship and deflation. The economy was not left to market forces; there had been the decree, already noted, ordering the reduction of all wages, of the prices of the industrial cartels and also of interest rates. The classical expectation had been that this would increase employment, but it had had the opposite effect. There was a slight episodic decline in the number unemployed and then a further sharp increase. By the early months of 1932, unemployment had passed the 6-million mark.

The other sectors of the economy – small enterprise and especially agriculture – were equally in distress. There are economic strains that democracy cannot survive; the fragile structure of the Weimar Republic was, as is commonly conceded, deeply vulnerable. Brüning was replaced briefly by even more desolate figures. For a desperate nation, Hitler and National Socialism soon seemed the answer, and, in narrow economic terms, they were.

Their solution was to close off the frontiers to imports and by rigid exchange control to arrest any flight from the mark, any loss of expansive effect to foreign sellers. Then domestic public expenditure was increased and men were put to work. (There was emphasis on men; women were expected to stay at home and concern themselves with church, children and cooking.) The public expenditure took a variety of forms; all involved borrowing, principally from the banks. In the beginning, the money went heavily into civilian public works, the most visible being the *autobahnen*. By 1936, the year of Roosevelt's reelection, the depression in Germany was, as noted, effectively over. Unemployment was at nominal levels. A step had already been taken in 1933 to guard against cost-push inflation: trade unions had simply been abolished. The further step was now taken of imposing a ceiling on all prices. Firms seeking more profit could expand production; they could not raise their prices.

In Germany in 1938 to learn at first hand of the course of German economic policy, I saw the Brown Shirts on parade and my contemporaries in military uniform. I heard the pervasive greeting: Heil Hitler! And I also heard professors and even an occasional government figure expressing their strictly private distaste for National Socialism and the Nazis. Nonetheless, I also saw an economic system in which reference to the depression was wholly in the past tense. There was a strong undercurrent of concern as to the way the recovery had been brought about, specifically as to the public borrowing and expenditure on which it so clearly depended.

But this was secondary to the general satisfaction that the country had escaped from the stark economic misery of earlier years.

The criticism of Germany in the centers of orthodox finance abroad, and especially in the United States, was much more eloquent. The German recovery was said, in all respectable comment, to be merely the prelude to a disastrous financial collapse. Hitler had set the Third Reich on a path that would destroy both him and the country's economy. Disaster did, indeed, await but not because of the economic policy.

One adverse economic aspect of the policies of National Socialism eventually did appear. The United States and Britain came to the Second World War with large reserves of available labor and plant capacity, while Germany came to it with no unused manpower and with an economy at the highest level of civilian production. For the United States and Britain, as also for Canada and the other British Commonwealth countries, the war meant expanded plant utilization and employment. For Germany it meant deprivation and an economically far from efficient resort to foreign and slave labor. The reservoir of unemployed workers and unused resources created by the depression was to prove a major source of wartime strength for the western Allies. To this I will return.

Two other countries, both small on the world scene at the time, deserve mention for the way they dealt with the depression. Japan suffered severely from 1930 to 1932; the world depression settled on the Japanese islands, and particularly on Japanese agriculture, with force. One consequence was marked political unrest in that characteristically well-ordered land and some actual violence. By the mid-1930s, however, recovery was well under way, and here, too, there was, essentially, full employment by 1936. Devaluation of the yen helped keep Japanese exports cheap on the world markets. More important was government support to the economy, namely by politically regressive expenditures for armament production and war. There was also the seizure of Manchuria in 1931, its costly establishment as the nominally independent state of Manchukuo three years later and thereafter the war with China. Because of the well-established Japanese association between government and industry, the expansion of Japanese industry was also publicly encouraged and supported. There was a retreat from the once-dominant role of textiles, followed by a substantial industrial investment elsewhere. Here, too, the breaking of the depressive equilibrium by public action.

A smaller and politically and socially much more benign attack on depression was that of Sweden. This too I saw at first hand as I came to know a remarkable group of Swedish economists – Gunnar Myrdal, Bertil G. Ohlin, Erik R. Lindahl, Erik Lundberg and Dag Hammarskjöld – who had broken with an earlier conservative tradition and concluded that mitigation of the depression's hardship and unemployment could come only from affirmative government action.

What they proposed, along with substantial currency devaluation, was government borrowing and public employment, with the promise of more conservative finance upon recovery. They believed in support to farm prices and a greatly strengthened social security system – old age pensions and unemployment compensation.

This program was carried into effect early in the decade of the 1930s, well before the word from Keynes. Nowhere else were economists so influential as to practical policy. Indeed, to a substantial extent, the Swedish economists, who were active in public affairs, *were* the policymakers. By the latter part of the decade the depression was over in Sweden because of their actions. From Keynes one had the theory; from the Swedes one had the intensely practical – and democratic – experience.

Nor did the Swedish recovery depend on armaments and war. Personal observation of what was being accomplished in that small country in this period was one of the most instructive and civilizing experiences an economist could have had. In a just world, reference would be not to the Keynesian but to the Swedish revolution.

12

The Second War

In the economic life of the United States during the Second World War, three matters stood out. First, as I've just said, there was the decisive economic advantage accorded by the huge reserves of plant and manpower created by the depression that could now be brought into use for military purposes and the broad support of the wartime economy. This was true also in Britain, Canada and Australia. The Axis powers were not equally fortunate. Depression had its unplanned and unexpected gift.

The second controlling factor, one also already indicated, was the strongly felt need to avoid the evident economic errors of the First War and their consequences. Particularly to be avoided was inflation and its aftermath. In the United States, the memory of the doubling of prices twenty years earlier was still vivid. And there was the well-recorded reminder of the German and Austrian hyperinflation and later disaster. The prevention of inflation became central to wartime attitudes in all countries.

Finally, there was the need to organize the procurement of the vast amounts of war materiel – the ships, planes, guns, ammunition, uniforms – and to make room in the civilian economy, where necessary, for this production. The wartime histories of this undertaking in the United States are seriously clouded because good fortune and undoubted intelligence and vigor were combined with marked incompetence, resistance and lassitude. The story of the latter has never adequately been told; it is something of which all who were of any perceptive tendency in Washington at the time were greatly and gravely aware.

In the autumn of 1939, with the Nazi invasion of Poland, war became inevitable, and in the following year, with the fall of France, American involvement became at least probable. It was out of the then-idle manpower in the United States, the women newly entering the labor force and the industrial plant either less than fully used or available for expansion that the war was supported and, as to materiel, eventually won.

In these years, under the initiative and guidance of Simon Kuznets, a quiet, unassuming scholar of great initiative and competence, there first became available an important statistical design, one which has now become a commonplace: the Gross National Product. This was an assessment of the total annual production of goods and services in the economy. From these calculations came a measure not only of what the economy was doing but of what it could do. And therefrom emerged a perception of how much military production was possible.

To those of us then involved, the Kuznets work was a guiding ray of light. Between 1939 and 1944, total production of American goods and services nearly doubled; the increase in constant dollars was from $320 billion to $569 billion. The civilian economy did not suffer; the vast claims of war notwithstanding, civilian consumption increased from $220 billion to $255 billion.[1] Some goods — automobiles, their tires and gasoline, other metal products, some textiles — were, of course, unavailable or in reduced supply, and there was a shift of consumption from the comfortably situated to the previously unemployed. In the aggregate, however, Americans finished the war better provided for than ever before. A decisive statistic explaining this good fortune was unemployment. In 1939, that stood at 17.2 percent of the civilian labor force; by 1944, it was down to a strictly nominal 1.2 percent.[2] Not before in American history had there been so much talk of sacrifice for the national good and, overall, such improved economic well-being.

The memory of World War I centered, as I've said, on inflation. Therefore, beginning with the first steps toward rearmament after the fall of France in 1940, there was concern that prices might get out of hand. The supremely irrelevant metaphor at the time was that having a little inflation was like being a little pregnant, this in a world in which abortion was unmentionable. In fact, a little inflation can be aborted, but that could not be said.

In the summer of 1940, I was called to Washington by Lauchlin Currie to take a hand in the early and elementary steps toward a price policy for which Leon Henderson, an energetic original New Dealer, was given general responsi-

1. These figures are from Galbraith, *Economics in Perspective*, pp. 247–48. They are in 1972 dollars.
2. Ibid., p. 248.

bility. Prices still being depressed and stable, there was little to do. I occupied myself with the problem of where the new defense plants should be located and under what auspices. There was special resistance from the business executives newly in Washington to giving the Tennessee Valley Authority – the socialist TVA – responsibility in this matter. My task was to counter these attitudes and encourage the location of new plants not where there was already industrial congestion but in rural areas, especially in the South. On this I was reasonably successful. Then the following spring, as prices began to rise and added impetus came from the White House to control them, I was placed in charge of the whole price-control effort.

At the end of 1941, after the attack on Pearl Harbor, the Congress gave full authority to the President to set prices and impose penalties for violation, some politically sensitive farm prices excepted. With these exceptions all prices were placed under a general ceiling – the General Maximum Price Regulation – in April of 1942. I remained in charge until the summer of 1943. The price controls remained in effect until the summer of 1946, a year after the end of the war. Rents were firmly controlled – a control it was to be difficult to abandon in New York City and elsewhere when the war ended. Wages were also subject to a less abrupt negotiated restraint.

Supplementing the price controls was a fairly comprehensive system of rationing that extended to canned goods, meats, sugar, shoes, automobile tires and notably gasoline. This involved a massive administrative effort of considerable originality and was the natural counterpart of price control. Where supply was exceptionally short and need exceptionally great, demand was thus brought forcibly into equilibrium with supply. The retail price index rose a total of only 29.5 percent in the entire period between 1939 and 1945. There was a marked bulge in 1946 when the controls were lifted, but the memory of the World War II years, unlike that of the earlier, and for Americans much shorter, conflict, is not of inflation.

It had been to prevent the social discomforts and discontents of inflation that the price controls were primarily created, but, in fact, they had another, less intended but, quite possibly, more important effect. As the demands of war procurement converged on the economy, there were two possible designs for enhancing return, for increasing profits. One was to raise prices; the other was to expand production. The price controls and associated wage restraints made the increase of production the only available course. Profit maximization, not a subordinate goal in wartime, was served horizontally by more production, not vertically by higher prices. Though not greatly noticed at the time, the price and wage controls had a strongly functional role in expanding wartime production.

None of this is to say that either the policy or the performance as regards prices and rationing was perfect. Much too much attention was paid to meticulous detail as opposed to overall result. This manifested itself in an undue concern for quality deterioration – too few peas in a can of peas, diminished durability in the rayon hose now replacing the unavailable silk. Politically damaging also, no doubt, was an arrogant certainty of high purpose on the part of the administrators, not made more attractive, considering the weight of the task, by their obvious youth. I was a well-recognized and politically celebrated case in point. It was the remarkable achievement of the civilian controls that they were economically successful, popular with the public but, in their administration, politically offensive.

The price and wage restraint and rationing were only half of the larger strategy of economic policy. They were the microeconomic effort; there was also the control of aggregate demand, the macroeconomic effort. The first was the task of the Office of Price Administration; the second – tax and financial policy and monetary policy – belonged to the Treasury and the Federal Reserve.

To an unusual extent, monetary policy was simply set aside during the war. Interest rates were kept low; the Federal Reserve lending rate – the discount rate – was effectively frozen throughout these years at 1 percent. One of the exceptional and exceedingly wise decisions of World War II was to avoid any reliance on the dubious magic of monetary policy. The rewarding result was that the borrowing made necessary by the war was at minimal interest rates, and the eventual cost of the war was much less because of the much lower interest cost and the only modest reward to the rentier class.

Instead there was a strong fiscal policy, macroeconomic reliance on taxation and the sale of government bonds, which (it was hoped) would absorb income that would otherwise have been spent. These efforts were remarkably successful.

Of the total wartime expenditure of more than $311 billion in the fiscal years 1941–45, approximately 43 percent was covered by taxes. This was a far better showing than in the earlier war. The major instrument was the income tax, along with an excess-profits tax designed to recapture undue war profits. The top bracket of the income tax was raised to 91 percent, but – a later and highly convenient doctrine to the contrary – this did not visibly reduce the incentive to effort on the part of the relevant rich.

Of the spending not matched and neutralized by taxation, a notable proportion was saved. Aggregate savings climbed from 4.1 percent of income in 1939 to 16.7 percent in 1945. (In 1991, they were back to 4.1 percent.) Remembering the hardships of the depression and assuming they would come again, people held cash or its equivalent in unprecedented amounts. Unable to buy a car, they saved the money against the day they could.

The comparatively stable prices also helped encourage saving – the holding of liquid assets in one form or another. Had prices been rising, the decision would have been very different. Business firms, unable to undertake civilian investment, also accumulated reserves. All of this was to have a remarkable later effect. During the war years it was assumed, indeed taken for granted, that after the victory the depression would resume. It had lasted for the previous ten years; once the wartime stimulation was gone, economic life would return to its depressive norm. But, in fact, good years actually lay ahead, and basic thereto was the spending and investment of the wartime accumulations. It would be pleasant to record that this was foreseen, a product of perceptive postwar planning. Alas, it was not; economic success is unquestionably based on intelligent foresight, but it also frequently depends on unpredictable good fortune.

As noted, the microeconomic action emerged from the Office of Price Administration and the macroeconomic action from the Treasury. It is not to be assumed that there was a wholly amicable cooperation between the two. It was my strong, frequently voiced opinion, as the officer principally responsible for microeconomics, that the Treasury should do more. The Treasury similarly expressed doubt as to the firmness, even astringency, of my administration.

As to macroeconomics, I was attracted, as were many others, by the idea of forced personal savings put forth by Keynes, whom I first came to know in person in these years and with whom, on infrequent occasion, I discussed my controls and the larger economic issues of the time. In return for a special levy under the forced savings plan, the citizen would receive a bond cashable and spendable after the war. Though pressed, the Treasury did not respond to this sugges- tion; it was a highly plausible proposal, but it was not accepted. Nonetheless, both the immediate and the longer- run effects of the principal economic policies of the war, the microeconomic controls and the macroeconomic taxation, were more successful than, indeed, we believed they would be at the time.

The further and central requirement of the war economy was, as noted, the procurement of tanks, aircraft, ships, guns, munitions and uniforms and the making of the necessary room in the civilian economy for this production. There was not enough steel for both automobiles and tanks or enough aluminum for both cookware and airplanes. Rubber was desperately scarce and in time also gasoline. Civilian use had to be curtailed, the supply of raw materials increased or both.

The procurement was handled with general competence by the armed forces. The army procurement was under the command of two highly qualified officers, Brehon Somervell and Lucius Clay, whose aptitude and experience went far beyond military drill and tactics. Somervell had previously handled WPA operations in New York for the New Deal, and Clay was later to achieve major distinction as the commanding American presence in postwar Germany. With the potential of the American economy before them, as shown by Kuznets and Robert Nathan, his onetime student and now his strongly motivated superior in office, they established the specifications and let the contracts for the required arms and equipment.

If the contracts thus granted turned out to be unduly generous, there was provision, in the form of renegotiation, to take back the excess return. If there was more forthright appropriation or graft, it was brought to public attention by a committee of the Congress headed by Senator Harry S Truman.

On the whole, the vast procurement operation was both efficiently conducted and remarkably devoid of profiteering and theft. There was, however, a less attractive side.

The making of room for this procurement – the ensuring of a supply of materials, their allocation from civilian to war use, the expansion of plant capacity, the closing down of civilian plant with competitive claim on materials and manpower and a great array of related activity – was, with some exceptions, handled with marked incompetence. The fact that a succession of alphabetical agencies had to be put in charge – the National Defense Advisory Commission (NDAC), the Office of Production Management (OPM), the Supply Priorities and Allocation Board (SPAB) and finally the War Production

Board (WPB) – advertised the failures and frustrations in the handling of these tasks.

The problem was political rather than economic. It was necessary to call on business executives for assistance; to mobilize industry without according a major role to business-men was unthinkable. Unfortunately, the business executives so brought to Washington had a seriously divided but politi-cally plausible view of their own purpose. Partly, needless to say, it was to further war production. To this some were devoted. But partly also it was to protect industry against Roosevelt and his now eight years of, as it was believed, antibusiness attitude and aggression. For many, the second task was not less urgent than the first. Coupled with this was the sad circumstance that often only the second-best business talent volunteered or was sent to work with the government. The best were actively engaged back at the home plant and office; those who came were individuals oriented not to operations but to business oratory and to past public and Washington advocacy.

That advocacy in particular had been against Roosevelt and the New Deal. Now, with the massive intrusion by govern-ment on industry, the need for care, caution and frequent resistance seemed greater than ever. Where strong initiatives were called for, there was a basic instinct for opposition.

Thus, well before the attack on Pearl Harbor, it was seen that more steel capacity would be needed. The great steel firms, however, did not want this – they had been living for a decade with excess capacity. Their resistance to expansion was strongly heard in Washington. Eventually it was to be small and new firms that took the lead in providing the increased production. Active industry resistance to shutting down the manufacture of automobiles after the war began was similarly reflected in Washington. Proposals for the allocation of scarce materials were met regularly with the answer: this can safely be left to the good sense (or voluntary cooperation) of the industry involved. During the years of preparation, and continuing after the entry of the United States into the war, there was a second, more pressing wartime conflict in Washington. That, for those of us then active in the New Deal, was with the advocates of firmly, even righteously, defended inaction.

In the end, those who promoted delay, voluntarism, inaction, did not succeed; the United States became, indeed, the arsenal of democracy. For itself and its allies, 86,338 tanks, 297,000 airplanes, 17.4 million rifles, carbines and side arms, enormous quantities of artillery equipment and munitions, 64,500 landing vessels and thousands of navy and cargo ships and transports were produced between July 1, 1940, and July 31, 1945, at a cost of $186 billion in then-current dollars.[3] By the end of the war, cargo vessels were being launched every twenty-four hours, and, as a slightly extravagant demonstration, the Kaiser shipbuilding yards in California built and launched an entire ship in just one day.

American industry in the war years had a curiously split personality. In Washington the well-advertised dollar-a-year men were the epitome of caution and even resistance. Out in the factories and shipyards, in contrast, one had a sense of great energy and initiative, a feeling of joyful revival from the years of depression, an enormous desire to show what this

3. Harold Underwood Faulkner, *American Economic History*, 8th edition (New York: Harper & Row, (1960), p. 701.

plant in particular, this country in general, could do. It was from the latter spirit and energy and not, alas, from those in Washington that came the great productive achievement of these years.

13

Britain and the Other Side

Although the enormous reserve of unused labor, plant and materiel was the decisive factor in the winning of the war, there was still much to be said for the positive aspects of American wartime economic performance. Much more can be said for that of Britain. Never before had a people so concentrated their energies as did the British after the fall of France. In Britain, as in the United States, the depression still endured, so there too idle manpower and plant could be brought into military employment. Now women went to work, and, far more than was the case in the United States, British civilian consumption was sacrificed to wartime need. Taxes were raised in the higher brackets to a level of near-total confiscation, and price controls and rationing, especially rationing, were put into effect over a wide range of consumer needs. Both the taxes and the rationing were accepted, even welcomed, with extraordinary good nature. The larger menace of Hitler loomed across the Channel; because of their sacrifice, all citizens could feel that they were participating in the common effort, were jointly doing their part.

In the United States, on the other hand, taxes (as ever),

price controls and, in lesser measure, rationing were much more controversial. No one administering the price controls could doubt the compelling desire for more money on the part of those so controlled. And rationing, especially gasoline rationing, was a source of no slight discontent and evasion. In Britain all these measures were accepted, and with little apparent outcry.

It has been sufficiently noted that the economic disasters of World War I became the lessons for World War II. No legacy of the First War was more continuously distressing than the debts to the United States, those of France and Britain in particular, that had been incurred for the purchase of war essentials. (On the similar problems posed by reparations payments, there is a word in the next chapter.) From the need to help the warring democracies and to forestall an eventual debt problem after the Second War came, in January 1941, the historic concept of Lend-Lease. Since debt would have unacceptable postwar consequences, and gifts or grants were semantically and thus politically too obvious, what remained was the notion that somehow aircraft, ships, raw materials and much else could be transferred to Britain and later in large amount to the Soviet Union, and that they could eventually be returned or repaid in kind. A clear distinction between lending and leasing was never made.

A sizable bureaucracy, of which I was briefly a member after leaving the OPA in 1943, was established in Washington to have oversight on the transfer of diverse weaponry and materiel and, in theory, to contemplate its later recovery. The latter transaction, needless to say, became lost in the vagrant recesses of public memory.

With the support of Lend-Lease but much more with that

of its determined citizenry, Britain became a formidable producer of weapons. Already in 1941 – a rather surprising matter – it was outproducing Germany in major military requirements, an advantage that it maintained throughout the following year. This was partly because the German wartime economic management was strikingly inferior and frequently incompetent, something I was to learn at first hand as the war was ending.

Having had a substantial role in American wartime economic planning and administration, I was recruited to help guide the postwar examination of the German economic performance. This was as a director of the United States Strategic Bombing Survey, an organization established at the suggestion of President Roosevelt and by order of Secretary of War Henry L. Stimson to ascertain the effects on the German and Japanese war effort of the Allied long-range or strategic bombing. This required a systematic look at all aspects of the enemy economies. The best in American (and some British) economic and statistical talent was assembled for this large-scale investigation and was in my charge in Germany. In the last days of the war my colleagues and I went with the American and British troops in search of the relevant German documents and personnel. There were many days of interrogation of high Nazi political figures from Hermann Goering on down, and notably of Albert Speer, who had been in charge of German economic mobilization and war production. It was an interesting, even privileged, exercise.

The German wartime economy centered at least partially on the lack of unemployed manpower and idle plant to draw into wartime production. Rearmament had begun in the late

1930s, but at a low level in relation to the eventual military requirements. Thus, as earlier told, the war found Germany with an economy at full employment and with a high civilian use of industrial capacity. Accordingly, the claims of war production had to be at the expense of the production of civilian goods.

As compared with those in Britain or even the United States, these claims were much more cautiously exercised. In the latter countries there was, traditionally, democratic communication between the people and the government. The government knew what the people could and would take. Given the mood in Britain after the fall of France and in the United States after the attack on Pearl Harbor, the will to sacrifice was strong, if in the United States more in rhetoric than in reality. In Germany there was no similar communication between people and state; the government, in consequence, was more circumspect in imposing sacrifice. This was one of the previously unperceived disadvantages of dictatorship.

At a very practical level and in combination with social, political and ideological constraints, women were not drawn into the German labor force. Nor, for that matter, were domestic servants, and their ranks were even augmented during the war by household help brought from the newly conquered lands to the east. Instead of a drastic cutback in civilian employment to staff the wartime factories, foreign labor was extensively and forcibly imported. To neither energy nor initiative was this work force strongly committed. German factories worked only one shift throughout the war, the shipyards and a few other enterprises apart. Here, too, peacetime custom prevailed.

The limited mobilization and employment were the result of Hitler's limited view of war. War was not something to be endured in a protracted fashion after the manner of the Western Front in World War I. Rather, the ruling military concept was of the blitzkrieg – a quick mobilization of forces, a powerful thrust, victory and submission, prompt demobilization. This worked with almost classical precision against the Low Countries and France in the spring months of 1940, and it was expected to work against Russia in the same way in 1941. The concept of the blitzkrieg also extended to the economic support behind the military campaigns. Arms production would be geared up to support the military thrust, and thereafter there would be relaxation and a return to the manufacture of civilian goods. Production was for short battles, not for a prolonged war. After the fall of France there was such relaxation, and this attitude continued to influence German wartime economic decisions. Only when the eastern blitzkrieg encountered the Russian winter and later the unexpectedly powerful Soviet armies was war production put on a permanent and determined basis. In consequence, arms production reached its peak only in mid-1944, and by then defeat, not victory, was increasingly the prospect.

Not all of the German performance can be attributed to its conceptual design or the previously mentioned problem that dictatorships have in gauging and mustering public response. High administrative incompetence was also to blame. Albert Speer, who took charge of German war production in February of 1942, was a man of intelligence and ambition, unhampered by any serious restraints of principle or conscience. Eminently available to Allied interrogators when the war was over, he acquired a reputation for his perceptive view of

National Socialism and his own achievements. He is today celebrated in history while far more important and more effective British and American administrators are not.

But Speer and a few others apart, the Third Reich brought to positions of authority men of decided economic and general inadequacy, ranging down to obtrusive incompetents. The by-no-means elementary problems of war mobilization and management were well beyond their grasp. Making a modestly revealing point under interrogation, Speer observed that many of those with whom he had to deal in the failing days of the war found escape from reflection on the developing disaster by remaining comfortably drunk.

The British and American wartime view of German economic mobilization was very different, and this had a striking bearing on military strategy and its effect. From the early years of the war there was a much-publicized reliance by the Allies on air attacks on German cities and on German industrial plants and rail transportation. The rationale of this warfare was economic. In the frequently heard American metaphor, the German economy was 'tight as a drum.' Any deletion of industrial plant would thus have an effect on total output and on war potential. And the effect on the war potential would become direct and compelling when war plants or shipyards as well as transportation were the targets. In fact, the air attacks, in some instances, helped force the Germans to mobilize into war use hitherto unmobilized resources, a fact made evident in the increased production of arms that continued up until the closing months of the war.

In the last days of February 1944, as a striking example of economic error, the German aircraft plants, the largest component of the arms industry, were the targets of massive raids. In March and later months, aircraft production rose enormously: 48 percent more fighter planes were produced in March than in February.[1] Factory buildings suffered heavy damage, but the basic machine tools came through mostly unscathed, and they were quickly put back into use. New assembly lines were organized in nearby buildings. The industry was also reorganized and moved from the incompetent direction of Goering and the Luftwaffe to the more efficient direction of Albert Speer and his ministry. Overall, the effect of the bombing was an increase in aircraft production.

The air attacks also brought the movement of resources from peacetime to wartime purposes – nitrogen from agriculture to munitions, gasoline from automobiles to aircraft and army vehicles. Even the attacks of the Royal Air Force on urban areas may have had a stimulating effect. The German air raids on London in 1940–41 were thought to have further heightened British morale. Not less, it was the conclusion of the Bombing Survey, 'the air raids of 1943–44 [on Germany], particularly the area attacks of the RAF, may have kept up the tension of national danger, and created the requisite atmosphere for sacrifice.'[2]

How much the air attacks raised morale can be debated; what is not in serious doubt is their larger economic effect. It was part of wartime doctrine that this would necessarily be great: economic strength was, as all knew, decisive. It was at the economy the bombers struck. In fact, the modern rich economy has a high measure of resilience. A dismaying

1. *The Effects of Strategic Bombing on the German War Economy*, United States Strategic Bombing Survey, October 31, 1945, p. 156.
2. Ibid., p. 26.

shortage in one area can be overcome by drawing supplies from a less essential use elsewhere. The long-range or strategic bombers did not win World War II; it is not clear that they even appreciably shortened the war in Europe.

One appeals here to the considerable service of history. In both the military and the associated civilian mind there is little that is more certain than the decisive role of air power. We have planes; therefore they must be effective. No doctrine is, in reality, so suspect. In the years after the Second World War, American control of the air over Korea and Vietnam was complete; this did not win or demonstrably affect the course of the wars in those countries. They were still fought and won – or lost – on the ground. In the aftermath of the minor operations in Grenada and Panama, there were grave misgivings as to the contribution of attacks by air and particularly as to the casualties they unnecessarily caused. Even after the Gulf war there has been substantial reappraisal of the accuracy and effect of the bombs. The belief in the efficacy of air power remains strong; the historical record is, at best, dim.

More generally, there is exaggeration and error when it comes to the role of economics in war and as a peacetime instrument of foreign policy. The purpose of the strategic bombers was, as noted, an economic one: it was to deny the armed forces vital economic support. This they did not do. Because of the affluent civilian production of the modern economy, there is not only an enormous opportunity for transfer from peacetime to wartime purpose; there can also be a less than fatal, maybe less than painful, sacrifice on the part of the citizenry. This accounts for the frequently minimal effect felt in modern times from sanctions, boycotts and embargoes. Since they do not involve the deployment of troops or other politically difficult or dangerous action, they are thought to be an attractive design for bringing recalcitrant governments to heel. Instead what occurs is a reallocation of resources and a sacrifice of nonessentials. With sanctions hope is great, disappointment endemic.

In World War II, responding to the presumed importance of economics and economic effect, more serious attention was accorded what was called economic warfare. In the United States, the Board of Economic Warfare, the BEW, was a highly prestigious organization headed by Henry A. Wallace, who was otherwise inadequately employed as Vice President. The hopes here too were great, the achievements negligible, and its very existence is now largely lost to history.

The Japanese wartime economy, to which I also gave study, was, indeed, well mobilized. The cartels, the great *zaibatsu*, lent themselves well to the task, and a disciplined proletariat also served effectively. Japanese mobilization was more comprehensive and astringent than that of Germany and, considering the resources available, far more so than that of the United States.

Japan, however, was still a small country with a relatively small industrial and resource base, and it was involved in a very large war. However well it used its industry for wartime purpose, this disparity was a controlling factor.

The air attacks on Japan, especially the devastating and inordinately cruel city raids, were more severe than anything Germany suffered. Japanese industry may also have been more vulnerable than German industry; in any case, the damage was less quickly repaired. Again, however, it was ground and naval warfare (together with the defeat of

Germany) that brought Japan's eventual surrender, not the economic loss of its military supplies through bombing raids.

The Japanese situation, it should be noted, was made worse by its highly adverse military and strategic situation — by the need to defend a territory extending deeply into the Asian mainland and along a long chain of islands down to Guadalcanal. This territory was vulnerable to what could be overwhelming attack on any link in the chain. The Strategic Bombing Survey concluded,[3] more than incidentally, that the atomic bombs advanced the end of the war by only a matter of weeks. The Japanese leadership had already accepted defeat; the decision to surrender was already in process.

One is reminded that in both Germany and Japan economic matters were subordinate to military and political decisions. The latter could be, and on occasion were, at a high level of incompetence, even insanity. Such, for example, was Hitler's decision to go to war with the Soviet Union and deploy forces over the vast Russian plain in the few months before the Russian winter. Likewise Japan's design for inciting a full and devastating American response by the attack on Hawaii. And, immediately thereafter, Hitler's declaration of war on the United States, thus ensuring that American attention and power would not be diverted in large measure from Europe to the Pacific. Any assessment of the role of economic decisions in the war must see them in the perspective of the far more destructive political and military errors. Again the primal role of stupidity in shaping the course of history.

3. *Japan's Struggle to End the War*, United States Strategic Bombing Survey, July 1, 1946.

14

The Peace, I

No country in modern times ever emerged from a war into such happy economic circumstances as did the United States in 1945. The budget was quickly cut back – from $92,690,000 in 1945 to $29,773,000 in 1948, a peace dividend of truly compelling size. In one of the more imaginative and civilized actions in modern history the soldiers released from active duty were offered the opportunity of paid schooling to compensate for the years missed while in the service. There was a large and more than grateful response.

In 1946, under heavy industry lobbying, the price controls were lifted, and there was, as already noted, a bulge in prices, but it soon somewhat subsided. Far more important, and at the time decidedly more surprising, was the performance of the economy as a whole.

All but universally, as earlier observed, the view of the postwar prospect had been dismal. Ten years of depression had preceded the war; who could doubt that depression was normal? Speeches were made telling of a better economic world to come, but these were thought the vacuous rhetoric that so often on economic matters is used to cover a harsh reality. The depression did not return.

The reasons for this are not, in retrospect, obscure. Remaining from the war years was the large reserve of unspent purchasing power previously discussed. Money that ordinarily would have gone for automobiles, other durable goods, housing, even some clothing, had effectively remained in hand – in cash, bank deposits or war bonds. Civilian investment had also been postponed. All of this formed the great reserve of purchasing power that now came to market. There was also a major paying down of the war debt; in 1947 and 1948, the federal government had surpluses of $3,862,000 and $12,001,000 respectively over expenditures of $34,532,000 and $29,773,000. Unemployment, which, as we've seen, was at 17.2 percent of the labor force in 1939, was at 3.9 percent in 1947. It had previously been taken for granted that the pain of war would be especially acute in its aftermath. This, in singular measure, was not the experience of the United States now. Never had things been better.

The impression, indeed fear, of hovering economic disaster did not entirely dissipate, but what now existed was the feeling that intelligent economic action could do something about it. That seemed a prime lesson of the war. The vast intervention of government and the expenditure and investment that produced the full wartime employment were the ultimate affirmation of Keynes. Now the conclusion: let the lesson so well learned have continued application.

The required action was associated with something nearly unparalleled in the history of economics: the new, wonderfully high prestige of economists. Professional economists had been prominent in the war mobilization. They had developed the new national accounts – National Income and Gross National Product, present and potential – and thus shown what war production was possible. They had been dominant in the creation of the microeconomic policy that controlled prices and restrained wages and the macroeconomic policy that taxed and restrained aggregate demand. Having served in war with evident success, they should, it was now clear, so serve in peace.

From this favoring attitude came the Employment Act of 1946. It was not a presidential initiative; under the primary auspices of Senator James Murray of Montana, it emerged almost spontaneously from the Congress. Initially entitled the *Full* (emphasis added) Employment Act, it was tempered down by conservative legislators and pressure. Modified were some original clauses asking that there be prepared each year a program of expenditure, taxation and other policy that would ensure jobs for all. Instead the bill created a special advisory group of economists that would be lodged in the White House to get the highest possible attention for progressive economic policy. A joint committee of the two houses of Congress would receive and, if only by publicity and persuasion, act on its messages. So were born the Council of Economic Advisers and the Joint Economic Committee. Professional economists would make up the Council and be strongly represented on the staff of the Committee. Implicit was the commitment to a broad policy of managed demand for high employment and vigorous economic growth.

Here, rather than in the mellowed-down requirements of the legislation, was the real force of the Employment Act. It put responsibility for macroeconomic management of the economy firmly on the government. Were there unemployment, unsatisfactory economic performance, it was henceforth the government's failure and the government's responsibility to do something about it. So it would be in the future for Democratic and Republican Presidents alike.

Initially President Truman reacted to the new legislation without enthusiasm. His first appointee as Chairman of the Council, Edwin Nourse, was a distinguished economist of the old school with no commitment to the new world of Keynesian economics. He had not, it was supposed, read Keynes. Soon, however, he was succeeded by Leon Keyserling, a lawyer become economist, a committed activist who was strongly allied with labor and the labor movement, and articulate, belligerent, often offensive. He was more than adequately firm in his belief in government support to the economy. Professional economists regretted that Keyserling did not have the appropriate professional credentials, but none could doubt his effectiveness. Under him the Council achieved an eminence in economic policy that was to be clearly manifest in the years to come. Full credit should also go to it for what could rightly be called the good years of American capitalism.

The economic difference between the United States, Canada and a few other fortunate countries and the devastated lands of Europe and Japan in the years after the war could hardly have been greater. There was, first, the physical destruction, which was evident in urban England, relatively slight in France, moderate in Italy and terrible in Germany and Japan and also in Eastern Europe and the Soviet Union. This was the legacy of both ground combat and, more particularly, the determined and extensively random destructiveness of air warfare.

The repair of this destruction in the erstwhile enemy countries was initially threatened by the reparations policy. Nothing, as noted, had more plagued the economic world after the First War than the reparations problem – the need of the defeated countries, Germany in particular, to find the money for reparations payments. This could only come from hard-currency reserves, which did not exist, or a sufficient excess of exports over imports. The effort was deeply disturbing to all normal economic intercourse. After World War II, it seemed obvious, the problem of reparations in cash must be avoided. Here again the voice of John Maynard Keynes; it was against this foolishness that he had warned after going home from Versailles.

Instead reparations would now be taken in kind, in shipments to the needful victors of coal and other requisites from the enemy countries and the taking of industrial machinery and equipment to replace what had been lost in the war. Thus would the winners' lost plant be replaced, their industrial production be got moving again. Reparations, to repeat, not in cash but in kind. Responding to a more imaginative and punitive mood, this would also take from Germany and Japan the economic basis of their war-making power; their peaceful behavior in the future would thus be assured. Especially in Germany reparations in kind served the broader concept of 'pastoralization,' the return of the country to the enforced peace of an agricultural existence. A version of this was known in Washington as the Morgenthau Plan for its most famous advocate, Secretary of the Treasury Henry Morgenthau, Jr.

Within months after the end of the war this imagery had to be set aside. However impossible reparations in cash, reparations in kind were worse, and in their social effect more demoralizing. As the official immediately responsible for German and Japanese economic affairs in the State Department in these months, I saw this with signal clarity. It was to be my principal effort during this period, aided by others who agreed, to bring this error to an end.

Reparations from Germany in the form of greatly wanted coal, for example, were possible only from a reasonably working economy – one that supplied to the miners the requisites of production and of life and, especially at the time, sufficient food. Industrial equipment taken in reparation was often of little value to the recipient country. It did not fit with the existing plant; needed replacement parts were not available, nor were the appropriate maintenance skills; much Japanese industrial plant was irrelevant for a less developed country such as, say, the Philippines. In Germany, where some industrial plant was removed by the Soviet Union, nothing was more dispiriting, even cruel, for the citizens of an already battered community than to see what they depended on for their livelihood dismantled by uniformed foreigners and carried away. Soon this policy was brought to an end in both Germany and Japan. It had been superior to reparations in cash only in that the error of the effort became more quickly apparent.

There was another lesson from these years, more important and imperfectly appreciated even in our own time. It is the radical difference between the military occupation of elementary agricultural territory and the taking over of a modern, intricately complex industrial society. The first is possible; the second is not only impossible but inflicts some of its heaviest burden on those who seek to do it.

Peasant, or even more modern farming territory occupied in the aftermath of military success has served or serves the victor about as well as it does the vanquished. Production continues; the basic decisions and the essential requirements of management are handled by the peasant or farm proprietor. Production beyond actual need is still sold; taxes are still paid or, as necessary, exacted. The new territory adds to the wealth and prestige of the conqueror. Even its manpower can be forced into service. The new ruler may be resented, but rule, and successfully, he can. So, as earlier told, it has been since the most ancient of times.

Modern industry and industrial life, in contrast, do not lend themselves to successful operation under military occupation and control. This could have been a lesson in the aftermath of World War I and the generally disastrous French occupation of the Ruhr. It was more than adequately evident in both Germany and Japan in the aftermath of World War II. The modern industrial economy is a creation of infinite complexity. There must be raw materials, components, skilled and unskilled workers, transportation, finance, attentive management and markets. And at every stage, in one form or another, there must be the demanding role of the state. Industry must have an autonomy that is inconsistent with military rule, and it must have government support that no military or foreign government can provide. In the months following the Second War the Allies quickly learned that the control of industrial production, and therewith the associated and essential government responsibility, had to be returned to the Germans and the Japanese. In September 1946, a little more than a year after the end of the war, Secretary of State James F. Byrnes, in a speech in Stuttgart, Germany, effectively returned the management of their own economic life to the Germans. I was present and listened to the address with both interest and approval, for I had drafted it.[1]

For the defeated powers autonomy and responsibility were, however, not enough. There had also to be working capital and the incentive to produce.

1. It was read and perhaps polished by Benjamin Cohen, counsel to Byrnes, and he later, no doubt rightly, took a measure of credit for it.

15

The Peace, II

Sufficient mention has already been made of the determination of the adversaries in World War II to avoid the economic errors of the First War. And, especially, of the determination to avoid inflation. To this end, prices were controlled, and food and other consumer essentials rationed. The rationing was mild in the United States and Canada, rigorous in Europe and Japan. Where it was severe, although this was little recognized at the time, it led to a different and even more stultifying form of inflation.

In particular, as money was borrowed and spent for arms and war, that money piled up behind the rationing system; there was little or nothing unrationed to buy. Available stocks of almost all unrationed products had yielded to the thought that any purchase was better than holding the nearly useless currency. And since money would not buy anything, why sell something in order to get it? Or why produce? Or work for it? This was the extreme case of a money-abundant, tightly rationed economy. It was closely approached in Germany in the years at the end of and just after the war, and, in lesser measure, it was the condition of the other warring countries in Europe and of Japan. In Germany, cigarettes, which, unlike paper money, were worth having and holding, became, to a considerable degree, the medium of exchange. Cigarette butts were retrieved and cherished. In a passageway leading to General Lucius Clay's headquarters office in Berlin was a men's washroom. On one wall was a printed sign: 'DO NOT PUT CIGARETTE BUTTS IN THE URINALS.' Beneath it a thoughtful G.I. had written, 'It makes them soggy and hard to smoke.'

The obvious solution was to diminish the regular currency outstanding by requiring the exchange of the existing notes for a smaller but functionally effective number. This, with characteristic pragmatism, the French did in the early months after the war. It had the further practical effect of denying to erstwhile black-market operators and those who had enjoyed special privileges under the collaborationist Vichy government any continuing advantage from their previous political reward; it was not wise to confess guilt by bringing in a currency hoard for exchange.

In Germany, where the situation was more serious, a proposal for a currency exchange was under consideration in American government circles as early as 1946. Two distinguished economists, Gerhard Colm and Raymond Goldsmith, both Americans of European origin, had joined with Joseph Dodge, a Detroit banker who was now concerned with German financial affairs, to draft the Colm-Dodge-Goldsmith Plan to achieve this end. In the State Department I was associated, if somewhat marginally, with the effort. The plan languished until 1948, when, in slightly more conservative form,[1] it was put into effect by German Economics Minister Ludwig Erhard.

There was a prompt and impressive reaction. Goods once held in preference to sale for the greatly redundant currency now came to market; shops previously barren suddenly filled up with things to buy; production for payment in money was now worthwhile. An everyday reference was to the Erhard miracle, the role of the original authors of the plan going largely unremarked. The 'miracle' would have been substantially less had it not been for a companion effort, which was also in marked contrast with the economic policy after the First War.

In the years following the surrender of the Germans and the Japanese, there was need to repair and otherwise rehabilitate the industries destroyed by military action. This, relative to other problems, was not too difficult a matter and was far less serious than was commonly supposed. As earlier noted, the actual destruction was much smaller than the devastated urban landscapes suggested and the accepted view of air warfare held. But there was also the less obvious fact that in the normal course of economic life much industrial equipment is always in the process of replacement in consequence of either obsolescence or wear. This had been observed a century earlier by John Stuart Mill and was an aspect of the 'creative destruction' in the capitalist process celebrated by

---

1. In its original design it had included a capital levy. Thus those who had fixed and immune wealth such as real estate would suffer along with those less fortunate who had liquid assets in the form of cash or bank deposits. The idea of a capital levy encountered fierce resistance from American conservatives; it was not the sort of thing the United States should propose or countenance. Perhaps it might be a precedent.

Joseph Alois Schumpeter. The war had merely accelerated that process. The physical destruction of industrial plant was far from the worst problem for postwar Europe or Japan.

A worse problem was how to get *and pay for* the working capital – the food, raw materials, machinery components, machinery itself and other requisites – that was essential for getting production under way. In the nature of the case, much of this had to come from the United States or in lesser measure from the other nations that were still capable of supplying food and raw materials. In either instance, dollars or their equivalent were needed to pay. These were not available in the needful countries and would not be available so long as there was nothing they could sell.

The plausible course was for the United States to lend in sufficient amount so that the devastated countries could buy the requisites for recovery. Here again, however, the earlier experience warned and intervened. An international debt load with debt service to be paid (and eventually forgiven) would thus be created, and this was precisely what Lend-Lease had been designed to avoid. There was only one solution; that was to *give* the money. And here entered the Marshall Plan. It bore the name of Secretary of State George C. Marshall, who, in proposing a helping hand for Europe in a Harvard commencement address in June 1947, may well have initiated a more impressive action than he then expected.

There had been an earlier, less celebrated response. In December 1945, after negotiations in which Lord Keynes was the dominant figure, a loan from the United States to Britain of $3.75 billion at 2 percent interest had been arranged. It was specified, in a formidable imposition of orthodoxy on

157

common sense, that sterling, its use hitherto under rigorous wartime control, would become convertible within one year of the conclusion of the loan agreement. And so it came about. This was a disaster. Those who, whether legitimately or unscrupulously, had accumulated sterling hoards during the war proceeded eagerly to convert them to dollars. A rich reward.

The loan proceeds were quickly dissipated; their effect on the British economy was minimal. This was a mistake that the Marshall Plan now sought to avoid. There would, on the whole, be a more cautious move back to normal economic life. Controls, including exchange controls, would, as required, be retained. Liberalization was the ultimate but not the recklessly immediate goal.

There was another, especially serious economic and political problem; this was the very delicate question of how the money made available by the Marshall Plan would be divided among the needy European claimants. A persuasive economic logic was brought to bear on this process; each country was asked to come up with a goal as to recovery, along with a calculation of the imports necessary to sustain progress toward that goal and the resulting balance of payments deficit. The latter deficit would then be covered by the Marshall Plan aid. (The story is told that the Turks first came up with balanced international accounts, believing that this would best impress the economically responsible Americans. They were rather sternly advised that under the new economic dispensation the course of wisdom was not to seek such a balance but to show a persuasive deficit. Over a single night the Turkish accounts were revised.) Serious attention needed also to be paid to how and for what the money was spent. To this end, sizable organizations in both Washington and Paris were created for what, without apology, was seen as essential economic planning – a planned recovery.

It is possible that the Marshall Plan and the considerable and prestigious role attached to its leaders – Paul G. Hoffman in Washington, W. Averell Harriman in Europe – and notably also to its economists disguised once again the deeper reality. The money was the thing. With that available, the rest followed. This, however, should not deny significant credit to the economists who helped decide how the money should be used.

Three greatly distinguished figures – Robert J. Marjolin in France; Eric, later Lord, Roll, stationed in Paris from Britain; and Richard Bissell in Washington – were in close professional communication. All put aside narrow national interest. Marjolin and Roll, it might be noted, went on to distinguished careers in their own countries. Richard Bissell continued his public service after the Marshall Plan in the Central Intelligence Agency, where he pioneered the development of the U-2 espionage plane. His career came to an end in a matter of hours in 1961, when he emerged as the individual principally responsible for the Bay of Pigs operation. A sad story.

The initial expenditures of the Marshall Plan were a little under $6 billion, and eventually about $13 billion in all (in present-day dollars a very substantial $53 billion) passed through the Economic Cooperation Administration (the ECA), the Washington agency established to oversee the program. A little more than half went for primary products – food and industrial materials – 17 percent for fuel, 17 percent for machinery and 7 percent for shipping costs.

The effect was all that could be hoped: in the three and a

half years of Marshall Plan operations, the Gross National Product of the countries assisted increased by 25 percent; industrial production went up by 64 percent and farm production by 24 percent.[2] Some of this would, of course, have occurred in the normal course of events, the difficulties notwithstanding, but since the recovery coincided with the work of the ECA and its impressive deployment of talent, the Marshall Plan inevitably received the major share of the credit. It stands in memory, as it did at the time, as the most successful of economic initiatives.

There was also a less publicized effect of the Marshall largesse. Much of the money so provided came back to the United States for the purchase of food, raw materials and capital goods. It was thus a powerful stimulant to the American economy, another of the supports to favorable performance in the postwar years. In economics, as, one trusts, in larger life, it is possible to do well by doing good.

That the Marshall Plan may be thought more important by historians than the reality would justify is suggested by the case of Japan. The devastation there was as great or greater than that in Europe. However, the Japanese government turned energetically to the task of restoring its battered economy, as did the *zaibatsu*. The latter were strongly in support of recovery, as were the smaller firms and the people as a whole. From this unified and determined effort came a recovery not less dramatic than that in Western Europe. It is an important comment on the relative importance of external help and internal determination.

*

2. Faulkner, *American Economic History*, p. 727.

There is no doubt that the Marshall Plan was motivated in no small part by goodwill and concern for both erstwhile allies and enemies. By 1947 and 1948, however, another factor was becoming strongly evident that would be economically important, even dominant, over nearly all of the next half century. That was the fear of Communism. In the war years the world had watched with awe and also with admiration and profound relief how the Red armies had met and thrown back the forces of Adolf Hitler. Some of their supporting armaments had come from Lend-Lease; more had come from an astonishingly powerful mobilization of Soviet economic resources, this despite vast losses to the enemy of territory, industrial equipment and raw materials.

Now, at war's end, all of Eastern Europe fell under the influence or control of the Soviet Union. The impression of formidable power was deepened by the dominating figure of Joseph Stalin, the last of the great Allied triumvirate of Roosevelt, Churchill and Stalin still active as leader of his country. The revolutionary aims of Communism, indeed its inevitability, had always been sufficiently celebrated, on the whole impressing conservatives more than they did the proletarian masses. When the Marshall Plan came into being, therefore, its creators were motivated both by an unselfish compassion for economically afflicted people and by a deep and insistent concern that the Soviet Union might otherwise occupy a depressed and vulnerable Western Europe. This union of goodwill and deep fear helped sanction the large monetary costs that were projected. Goodwill, which was undoubtedly present, would not have been enough.

In the years to come and particularly in the matter of help to the poor countries of the world, American economic policy would be influenced by a continuing combination of compassion, idealism and paranoiac fear of Communism. The idealists, those who backed loans and direct aid to the poor countries and even such mild enterprises as the Peace Corps, would be able to exploit the fear of Communism to gain the needed congressional approval and economic support. To this, a matter in which I was rather substantially involved, I will also return.

16

The Good Years

In the United States in the months after the lifting of price controls in late 1946, there was the sharp increase in prices already mentioned, making the war seem, in contrast, a time of relative stability. Thereafter there was considerable inflation, ranging from 8.5 percent in the consumer price index in 1946 to a high of 14.3 percent in 1947. Production was expanding and unemployment was very low. Demand was sustained not only by the release of the pent-up wartime purchasing power but by the strong merchandise balance of payments. American exports were greatly wanted; imports, and certainly those from Germany and Japan, were decidedly modest. Marshall Plan money, as already said, was flowing back to the United States to pay for American commodities and manufactures. The American economy was the pivot around which the world economy turned.

And so it was turning in 1948, when, unexpectedly, Harry Truman, after filling out the more than three and a half remaining years of Roosevelt's fourth term, was elected to his own first full term as President. The universally expressed surprise of his victory over Thomas E. Dewey should not have been so great: American voters do not react adversely to Presidents who preside over peace and prosperity.

The peace, however, did not last. In 1950, the invasion of South Korea by North Korea and our prompt intervention brought a brief run on consumer markets; there was recollection of the mild wartime shortages and price increases, along with the fear that there might be a return of inflation. This produced protective action, and by now the needed response seemed not in doubt. Congress supplied the necessary legislation – the Defense Production Act of September 1950 – and price controls were put back in place. The consumer markets once again became stable. Unemployment remained low; civilian living standards, with notable exceptions, continued to rise.

In 1953, the twenty years of Democratic presidential tenure came to an end. The Democratic administration, having earlier presided over an evidently necessary war, now found itself with an increasingly disliked one on its hands. This had been made more so by the spectacularly irresponsible behavior of General Douglas MacArthur, who invited the Chinese to intervene, suffered a crushing defeat when they did, urged a yet larger war and then was sacked from his command. Dwight D. Eisenhower and his promise to go to Korea and seek peace seemed a benign alternative. As Presidents are not defeated in good economic times, so they or their parties do not survive unpopular wars. Economic performance is central to political success, but to war such success can be deeply subordinate.

In the 1952 election campaign the Democratic candidate, Adlai E. Stevenson, was not strongly abreast of, as it was by now called, modern macroeconomics. His education at Princeton University had been in the earlier and astringently classical tradition: balanced budgets, the gold standard. The Keynesian notion that the government should, in times of serious unemployment, run a deficit to support the flow of aggregate demand he thought merely an excuse for unduly casual finance. A good government balanced its accounts at all times.

These beliefs did not, however, prove to be a grave short-coming. His economic speeches reflected the modern mood, for I wrote a large number of them. I did not therein minimize the role of fiscal policy in maintaining full employment, and although we indulged in some, mostly amiable, debate, Stevenson, if still in doubt, went along. Nor was this viewpoint seriously challenged by Eisenhower and other Republican speakers. Marx, by way of Joseph McCarthy, was a major voice in the campaign; the views of John Maynard Keynes had subsided into quite general acceptance.

In the favoring economic context and with the agreed-upon responsibility of the state to keep it so, much of this election, as would be the case in later years, was fought over social issues. Relatively soft restraint on trade union organization and the collective bargaining process – the Taft-Hartley Act – was a dominant concern. The farm program, the strengthening of Social Security, other social problems, dominated the economic discussion. The question was not the performance of the economy as a whole but how and to whom its rewards were to be distributed. To an extraordinary degree, it was accepted that the rich should pay in a substantial way from their good fortune. Marginal rates of the income tax were at 94 percent at their wartime peak; they were still at 92 percent in 1952. The adverse effect on incentives was little mentioned; given the favorable performance of the economy, a struggle to maintain after-tax income might, perhaps, have been stressed as a positive economic influence, forcing a greater managerial and entrepreneurial effort. In my years as an editor at *Fortune* magazine in the latter 1940s, this was once urged, but largely to annoy one or two of the more conservative members of the editorial board. During the campaign and in the early 1950s generally, it was help to the less fortunate – the welfare state – on which discussion centered. A favorable overall economic performance was more or less assumed. Dwight Eisenhower, taking office in 1953, was the least ideological of Republicans. The Korean war restraints were ended; little else was changed. The good times continued.

In Britain the Labour government moved cautiously to remove the wartime rationing and price controls. Only as increasing supplies were available was the market equilibrium restored. Meanwhile, as promised by Winston Churchill during the war and urged by the 1942 Beveridge Report, strong steps were taken to strengthen the welfare state and ensure the ordinary worker and citizen a decent minimum of well-being. From war service would come the peacetime reward. In the English-speaking world Britain became an accepted model in this regard.

In France, Germany, Italy and elsewhere on the Continent, a self-sustaining recovery continued as the Marshall Plan aid came to an end. In Western Europe, the first of the long-to-be-continued moves toward economic union were made with the establishment of the European Coal and Steel Community and the Benelux Economic Union. This was a civilizing action designed to improve economic well-being by the allocation of production across frontiers to the most efficient producers and also, and above all, to move on from the bitter nationalism that had produced the two wars with their accompanying death and deprivation. Great credit belongs to those leaders, most especially Jean Monnet of France and his close associate George Ball of the United States, who strongly pursued this vision.

However, no one should be in doubt as to the deeper motivation, a point again to be emphasized. Capitalism, as it matures, is basically an international system. Not only are its products traded across national frontiers, its enterprises also span those frontiers; the successful national corporation extends its plant and employment to other countries as a matter of course. Thus is born the transnational or international corporation. And thus diminished is its identification with any one country or government. A call for political union is, accordingly, in step with economic development; national identity and passion inevitably diminish with such development.

So do national tensions. The transnational corporation cannot stir up antagonism between two or more national states, for it is a presence in both and all. On the contrary, it looks for amity and the greatest freedom of movement of people, components and products. Communications, travel, finance, add to the sense of association. And workers look ultimately not only to their own government as their ruling force but also to the international entity by which they are employed and whence come their paychecks. It is the poor and less privileged who still respond to national and ethnic appeals. One of the still uncelebrated achievements of modern capitalism is that it takes many of its people beyond this narrow and potentially violent warlike situation.

In the years after World War II, conditions in Western Europe were the prime and rewarding example of the effect of this polar force. No one, to repeat, should deny credit to those urging political and/or economic unification, including those who called for it as a condition for participation in the benefits of the Marshall Plan. It was, nonetheless, their good fortune as well as their own good sense to be on the great tide of economic development. The latter, not the statesmen or the meetings and negotiations, was decisive.

In the 1950s, there was also recovery, if a less impressive one, in Eastern Europe and the Soviet Union. In 1958, I visited Poland and Yugoslavia to observe and to lecture, and the following year the Soviet Union, there traveling from Tashkent to Kiev and from Tbilisi to (as it then was) Leningrad. One could not but be impressed by the energy there being applied to industrial advance. And also by the highly visible results that the visitor was proudly shown. Progress was particularly evident as regards transportation, electrical generation, steel and large-scale industry generally.

There was good reason why such industry was given prominence. There calculation as to needed materials, components and manpower could readily be made, and the direction of operations could be carried out in a military manner. Planned production, in consequence, was both conceptually and practically possible. Because of this, as well as the tendency to see in steel mills, electrical installations, petrochemicals and the like the visible substance of economic progress, there was a marked emphasis and overemphasis on heavy industry in the Soviet Union and also its eastern satellites. Progress was less evident and celebrated in the consumer goods industries, where unstable consumer demand, the role of style and design and the multiplication of supporting services all made formal planning difficult or impossible. Failure there would one day be politically serious, even disastrous.

In light of later developments it would be personally gratifying to say that I foresaw the eventual and systemic failure in the Soviet consumer goods industries and also in agriculture. Alas, I did not. Rather, I was impressed by the Soviets' confidence that more would be accomplished and by the determination so expressed. In the United States touring economists were never expected to see the inside of a factory; in the U.S.S.R. we were asked daily to inspect one and to see how pridefully people worked or seemed to work. Only when we returned to the hotel to face distracted and sometimes indolent waiters, uncertainty as to what food on the menu might be available and a sense of surprise when the elevator arrived did we experience the lesser side of Soviet progress. On this I did not dwell.

Lurking always in good times are the seminal causes of less fortunate times to come. Prominent and already observed is the financial speculation that ensures the later crash. In the good times of the later 1940s and the 1950s were three sources of the distress that was soon to appear in the United States. The first was a revival of faith in the magic of monetary policy. In 1951, the Federal Reserve was released from its long wartime inactivity. Monetary action would again be used as a weapon against inflation and recession. Not to be relied upon in the serious exigency of war, it would again have a role in the less pressing problems of peace. No course of public action would be so successful in surviving disappointment about its efficacy and even its forthright failure.

These years saw also the strengthening of the trade unions and the sharpened juxtaposition of trade union and corporate power. And from this would come the threat of the wage-price spiral – wage demands pressing on prices, prices leading to new wage demands, the strong intrusion of microeconomics on macroeconomics as a cause of inflation. But not quite yet.

As the good years continued, it became evident in the industrial countries that the general well-being also had its darker side. In the United States there were the considerable number who did not share therein – those isolated in the valleys and hollows of the Appalachian plateau, in the rural South and in the densely populated urban slums.

Also increasingly evident was the disparity in what might be called the larger living standard. Private goods and services were wonderfully abundant, the services of the public sector much less so. Television was developing rapidly; many schools remained mediocre or bad. People lived in clean houses on filthy streets. Automobiles were highly styled and mechanically excellent; they were driven on highways that were made hideous by disorderly roadside commerce and commercial art. There was much more.

This imbalance in well-being and as between public and private living standards I celebrated in 1958 in *The Affluent*

Society.[1] The book and my carefully coined phrase 'the conventional wisdom' – the thought that attempted to justify this disparity in well-being – did not escape notice. Some millions of copies were eventually sold around the world, and the phrase passed into the language along with the title. Not much was changed thereby. The successful publication of a book has a strongly favorable effect on the author's psyche. And also, no doubt, on some of the readers. The larger social and political consequences can be difficult to see.

Finally in the good years, there was the revival of the Soviet economy previously mentioned and the economic, scientific, engineering and military power it would sustain and seem to sustain. On October 4, 1957, Soviet scientists and engineers put the space satellite *Sputnik* into orbit, to the surprise and considerable consternation of the American citizenry, not excluding the space scientists and engineers, who were well behind. These achievements of Communism impressed most those who loved that system least. Conservatives, especially in the United States, would thereafter be in thrall to both Communist success and its worldwide appeal and threat. From this would come continuing pressure for peacetime military expenditure, the arms buildup, the space race and the by-no-means-minor consequences of the Cold War.

1. Boston: Houghton Mifflin.

17

Decolonization, Economic Development

The years after World War II brought one of the more spectacular political developments of the twentieth century. That was the general shedding of their colonial possessions around the globe by the European states and by the United States: India by the British; the Philippines by the United States; the Middle East by Britain and France; Africa by Britain, France, Italy, Spain, Belgium and eventually Portugal; Indonesia by the Dutch; Vietnam by the French; Korea by the Japanese. Lesser islands and territories were accorded independence by these nations and others.

In common doctrine, there were two reasons for this change. There was a wise and compassionate recognition in the advanced industrial countries that the erstwhile possessions had a natural right to their own identity, to govern themselves. And there was greatly insistent pressure on the part of the colonies themselves for independence, something that had become too strong, too costly, to be resisted. The practical course was to let the brothers go in peace.

All this was doubtless true; there was, however, another,

less recognized and, quite possibly, more decisive factor: the colonies no longer rendered any justifying economic advantage. Once they had. They were a rich source of raw materials and varied consumer products. In return, they were a significant market for elementary manufactured goods. Those who so traded were economically and politically powerful. Lenin could say, if with considerable exaggeration, that the workers in the capitalist countries lived on the backs of the people in the colonial lands. And, with all else, there was the ancient commitment to landed territory as essential to the possession of wealth and power.

This was the case no more. The engine of economic well-being was now within and between the advanced industrial countries. Domestic economic growth – as now measured and much discussed – came to be seen as far more important than the erstwhile colonial trade. The colonial world having thus been marginalized, it was to the advantage of all to let it go.

The economic effect in the United States from the granting of independence to the Philippines was unnoticeable. The departure of India and Pakistan made small economic difference in Britain. Dutch economists calculated that the economic effect from the loss of the great Dutch empire in Indonesia was compensated for by a couple of years or so of domestic postwar economic growth. The end of the colonial era is celebrated in the history books as a triumph of national aspiration in the former colonies and of benign good sense and goodwill on the part of the colonial powers. Lurking beneath, as so often happens, was a strong current of economic interest – or in this case disinterest.

*

The colonies having gone, there did remain a sense of responsibility for their well-being as well as for the lands, like those in Latin America, that had experienced decolonization in earlier times. The rich countries in their evident affluence now accepted that they had some obligation to the poor. They should help and guide them to a similar, if perhaps lesser, well-being. So in the age of decolonization the idea of economic development was born. At one time the colonies had been left to their own stable poverty. Now, with independence, they too should advance.

Indeed, the first steps were taken before the war ended, when, in 1944, at the Bretton Woods Conference the International Bank of Reconstruction and Development (the World Bank), with a capital of $9 billion, was planned, along with the slightly smaller International Monetary Fund. The first was to provide the money for investment in the hard plant of economic development; the second, more diverse and less specific in its tasks, would help countries, new and old, to overcome the deficit in their balance of payments — the excess cost of imports over the exports associated with development — and specify the internal economies and discipline that, with prayer and hope, would correct the imbalance. The Bank and the Fund, both located in Washington, would bring the world of reputable finance into intimate association with the tasks of economic development.

And there was further action. The United Nations was, from its beginning, greatly concerned with economic improvement for its poorer members, as were its specialized agencies; discussion of the problem, often replacing action, was extended and intense. And similarly concerned was the

United States. In 1949, in his inaugural address, President Truman proposed assistance to the poor countries – the Point Four program. In the years following, this developed into the still continuing aid programs, which were encouraged during the Cold War by the hitherto mentioned conjunction of compassion and fear of Communism.

In 1951, responding to these changes, some younger colleagues and I began to notice the considerable number of students at Harvard from the poor countries who were studying the sophisticated and, for them, often irrelevant models of the modern advanced economy. We initiated a course in the economic problems and, we hoped, their solution in the countries whence the students came. It was one of the first such courses in the economics of poverty and economic development in the United States. Thereafter, while studying and writing on these matters in Puerto Rico, elsewhere in Latin America, and in India, Pakistan and Ceylon, as it then was, as well as while serving as Ambassador to India, I came to focus serious attention on the problem of mass poverty and the designs for escape therefrom. In India I had the ultimate responsibility for one of the largest and most ambitious of our efforts in economic development, by then denoted the AID (the Agency for International Development) program.

There were some notable successes in this overall endeavor. There was great progress along the Pacific Rim, as it is called, in Korea, Taiwan, Singapore and later in Malaysia and Thailand. Improved agricultural technology and irrigation and support to farm prices helped India become self-sufficient in its food supply and, rather more remarkably, to remain so while its population more than doubled. Elsewhere there were successful efforts to provide some of the rewards of modern economic life.

In general, however, progress has been deeply disappointing. Over the world as a whole, while the rich countries have gotten richer, most of the poor have remained desolately poor. The difference between rich and poor has remained great and, indeed, has increased. The assistance programs have done something to serve the conscience of the fortunate; they have done much less to lessen despair. Those countries just mentioned that have flourished, those on the Pacific Rim especially, have done so because of their own internal dynamic. This, not foreign assistance, has been the moving force. Where that internal energy, discipline and organization have been lacking, the aid programs to relieve the poverty of the masses have had little effect.

They have had little effect because of the failure to see economic development as a process with its own controlling parameters. This error was shared by the poor countries and the rich. The first requirement for economic development in any country is an educated and, in consequence, a competent and socially and economically motivated population. The importance of this was fully recognized in the early years of the now-advanced industrial countries. Free and compulsory education was then seen as a prime requisite of economic progress.

Also originally taken for granted in the rich countries was the need for internal tranquillity under a stable, responsible and minimally honest government. This was an accepted basis of, as it was then called, economic progress. It is still true now that nothing is more damaging to successful development than incompetent, irresponsible and corrupt government; nothing brings development more effectively to an end, indeed so effectively reverses it, as internal conflict.

One of the great errors in history has been the belief that the new nations would proceed naturally and even easily from colonial rule to a secure self-governing system. A transition of almost incredible complexity could, it was thought, be accomplished, a few politically advanced countries such as India apart, with a minimum of preparation or none at all. Stable democracy would come more or less automatically. That confusion, political conflict, domestic aggression, economic stagnation and deterioration and diverse human slaughter would be the alternative to colonial rule was not foreseen.

In modern times virtually all of the rich countries live at peace with each other. The poor, having nothing to lose, do not. Tribal conflict is exacerbated by poverty. So is religious conflict. In the rich countries political voice is, in some measure, earned by economic and related cultural and educational achievement. In the poor countries there is no such process; power can be possessed all too readily by the stridently vocal and pathologically ignorant.

In close and contributing association with the adverse circumstances within the poor countries have been the errors of the helpful rich. The first was to assume that what physically existed in the advanced economy could be passed on to the poor, and the latter would then be economically developed. Steel mills, electrical generating works, chemical plants, the other heavy furniture of developed capitalism, should be so transferred, and development would thus be accomplished.

This too was deeply in conflict with reality and need. Poor, unskilled and illiterate people needed food, clothing and elementary medical care. Instead they got factories and glossy airports that were less than relevant to their everyday lives.

Closely involved with these matters in India, I was constantly impressed by the tendency in individuals of the utmost goodwill to assume that their own particular American interest or occupation was uniquely appropriate to the local scene. If he or she was an expert in the United States in business management, poultry husbandry, home economics or veterinary medicine, this automatically achieved relevance in India. There are many types of imperialism; that which expresses the importance of personal competence or enthusiasm is not the least intrusive in effect.

There was a larger error. That was to see the economic and social systems of the advanced countries – market capitalism, socialism *cum* Communism – as competing developmental designs for the poor countries. In the poor lands and in the early stages of development, both capitalism and socialism are supremely irrelevant; the educated human talent and the public discipline for either are simply not available.

The belief that socialism was possible was especially damaging. In various countries this created a top-heavy apparatus of government initiatives, permissions and controls that were inimical to development. In India agricultural production, left largely to producer initiative once fertilizer, grain hybrids and irrigation were made available and with prices assured, was, as earlier observed, wonderfully successful. Industrial progress, on the other hand, was under the heavy burden of government controls, these aimed at achieving a social pattern of development. Supporting the controls was the fear of a new colonial regime under the rule of the transnational corporations. In recent times there has been movement toward the liberalization of Indian industry – toward lifting the onerous and comprehensive controls of the state. That, in turn, has encountered resistance, principally from the comfortably entrenched bureaucracy, which enjoys modest revenues from allowing exceptions to the regulations it administers. The sale of indulgences did not end with church reform.

In other countries the concept of a social design for development led to a positive discrimination against the agricultural or peasant population. Industrial development is urban in character; its work force is the proletariat on which social action centers. From this came the simplistic decision, especially in Africa, to keep agricultural prices low by public action as a favor to the urban masses. And from the low food prices and the impaired incentives came low or lowered agricultural development and food shortages. In the larger process of economic development, agriculture, which meets the rather elementary need for food and also some clothing, should have a primary, not a secondary, place. That, too, was once the acknowledged experience of the now-developed lands.

And this is not all. The feudal classes that had earlier so inhibited economic progress in the more favored part of the world remained in authority in the more unfortunate of the poor countries. So it was in the Philippines, in much of Central and some of South America, in Pakistan and elsewhere. Those so empowered do not especially want development;

instinctively, if not objectively, they see it as a threat to their own political position and economic well-being. In this context economic progress is not to be expected. Development requires the disestablishment of the landed oligarchy. To ask that, however, is to call for a revolution. Perhaps it would provide the opportunity for Communism. For these reasons it could not be urged. What remained was continuing talk of economic progress and an acceptance of economic stasis.

Further, as a deeply adverse factor, there has been the military nexus. As has already been stressed, the aid effort in the years after World War II was motivated by two things: decent compassion and the deeply rooted fear of Communism. The latter called for support to economic development; even more urgently, it called or seemed to call for military support and, on occasion, military intervention.

The result was unqualifiedly adverse for economic progress. Military aid replaced civilian economic aid. The poor countries were encouraged to divert internal resources to the military and scarce external resources – export-earned hard currency – to weapons purchases. An enormous trade in military artifacts resulted, and this trade bore in on civilian commerce and civilian need. In many countries it also brought military or militarily controlled governments into power. These were well designed to misunderstand or ignore the requirements of economic development. Or to find alliance with feudal power in effective resistance to economic progress.[1]

*

1. This point is impressively made by Ruth Leger Sivard. She is the author of

There was also in the poor lands the population explosion. Few social issues have been more discussed; its causes are reasonably evident. There is the basic sex urge, possibly enhanced by the absence of the competing diversions and recreations of the more advanced society; there is also the control of malaria, typhoid fever, venereal diseases and other forms of human devastation, AIDS being the principal exception; and there is the elementary mathematics of demography that allows two parents to reproduce themselves severalfold. All are relevant.

A further cause became apparent to me in my years in India: what is economically highly rational and relevant for the parent or parents is at odds with the social purpose. Offspring in the poor rural community are the basic protection against the trials of early old age. Children are there to endure the sun, heat and toil when the time comes for their elders to seek rest and shade. To be childless on a peasant holding is truly to risk the perils of one's later years. This is especially so if a landlord has the right of removal.

In India the birthrate is far lower in the cities than in the rural areas where some three-quarters of all the population live. There and in other peasant lands sons, with their superior muscular power, have, in the frequent case, been much preferred to daughters. (The latter in China and elsewhere were once disposed of at birth as an unwanted burden.) We have here the reason why the urgings of family planning and contraception have had minimal effect in poor

---

the indispensable *World Military and Social Expenditures, 1991*, which is, at this writing, the most recent of her annual reports on this subject. I am privileged to serve on her advisory board.

---

rural communities. And why, with continuing poverty, they will so continue.

There is always danger in generalization. In the years since decolonization there have been some very substantial examples of economic development. Those of Korea, Taiwan and the other Pacific countries have been noted. The Indian agricultural achievement, sometimes called a miracle or the green revolution, has also been mentioned. China has survived socialism and entered upon a period of rapid development, although not without recourse to market-inspired incentives.

In recent times there has been some recognition of earlier error. The great industrial incubus is now less seen as the basic symbol of economic progress. The importance of education is more widely understood. One of the enemies of economic development, indeed of civilized society, has been the notion that national sovereignty is sacrosanct even when it protects the internal conflict that destroys the economy and the people themselves. The community of nations, however reluctantly, is coming to recognize that this is so; action by the United Nations to intervene against civil conflict, if still uncertain and exiguous, is achieving a certain acceptance.

Stable government is a prime essential of economic development. So are education and increased agricultural production. These are the pivots on which successful development turns. Slowly and painfully, these matters are, one hopes, being recognized. We are still, nonetheless, at the beginning of a long and tortuous path.

18

The Kennedy Initiative

I now return to the United States and to a word on my long association with John F. Kennedy, particularly as this had to do with economics. Our personal acquaintance began in the 1930s, when he was a student at Harvard and I a relatively young instructor; most of our relationship at that time was through his older brother, Joseph P. Kennedy, Jr., who was then also a Harvard student, and through the sons I met their father.

J.F.K. and I were separated during the war years but came together to discuss economic and political matters when he became a congressman and then a senator. I was never a major speechwriter for him as I was for Stevenson; a younger generation of craftsmen had taken over. I was, however, called on to lend a hand with some frequency.

I did have more than a little to do with the economic positions he took. On these, oddly enough, I had the occasional support of Joseph Kennedy, Sr. Once, in New York, while I was preparing a speech for J.F.K. to give before economic editors and reporters from the local press, the elder Kennedy supported me in a rather more liberal position than his son was inclined to take. In a half-serious mood the President asked afterward, 'What the hell hold do you have on my old man?'

Kennedy did not take advice on economic matters casually. He sought diligently to understand the issue or issues under consideration; somewhat exceptionally, even idiosyncratically, for a politician, he gave every indication of enjoying economic discussion and the occasional intense debate.

In the last years of the Eisenhower administration, there had been a modest increase in prices, a consequent sharpening of interest rates by the Federal Reserve. There was an appreciable increase in unemployment from 4.3 percent in 1957 to 6.8 percent in 1958. There was then a drop in 1959 to 5.5 percent, where it remained in 1960, the election year.[1] This seemingly somewhat uncertain performance was thought, not least by Richard Nixon and his political associates, to be the cause of his defeat at the polls, thus ending the eight years of Republican presidential rule. It was not that serious; in the greater likelihood, the effect was too small to have much to do with the election result. The decisive fact was that Kennedy was personally and politically a far more attractive figure than Nixon. Economic issues did not much intrude on the choice between them. This did not diminish the role of economists and economics in the new government.

On the contrary, not before and not since have professional economists been so influential in public policy as in the administration of John F. Kennedy and continuing on into

---

1. *Economic Report of the President* (Washington, D.C.: U.S. Government Printing Office, 1993), Table B-38, p. 391.

that of Lyndon Johnson – specifically, Walter W. Heller from the University of Minnesota, James Tobin of Yale University and Kermit Gordon of Williams College. Heller and his associates on the Council of Economic Advisers were scholars of high academic distinction and a strong practical orientation. Enjoying the confidence of the President, they dominated the making of economic and related political policy.

In the White House in the first months after Kennedy's inauguration, later from India and on frequent visits to Washington therefrom, I was something more than an onlooker in the discussion of economic policy. The decisive power, needless to say, lay with those more directly involved.

There were three essential problems facing the Kennedy economists, some that had already been experienced and have been mentioned, and all no doubt clearer in retrospect than they were at the time. There were, first, the relative roles of macroeconomic and microeconomic policy. And within macroeconomic policy was the question of the respective roles of monetary and fiscal policy. And within fiscal policy the question of public expenditure versus taxation. All were subject to intense but, on the whole, remarkably civilized discussion.

The macroeconomic versus microeconomic debate, to remind, concerned the control of inflation. Inflation at the better levels of economic performance can be caused macroeconomically by the aggregate demand for goods and services pulling up prices. It can also be caused microeconomically by wage demands pressing up prices and higher prices stimulating wage demands – the wage-price spiral.

In the professional view of overall economic policy,

macroeconomic policy – the management of aggregate demand – enjoys high respectability. Microeconomic policy in its effort to mitigate or tame the wage-price spiral does not, and especially not in the English-speaking economic tradition. In one form or another, it requires interference with market behavior, with the undisturbed setting of prices and wages in the marketplace. The market, in turn, is sacrosanct in reputable economic attitudes, and even theologically less confined economists are reluctant to intervene. Nonetheless, in an economy of strong corporations and strong unions – still the clear institutional pattern in the 1960s – wages and prices did interact to cause inflation. This is not the classical conception of the free market, and it might justify public intervention. Accordingly, wage-price interaction was ignored or thoughtfully suppressed in much of the reputable discussion. There was thus a grim collision between the preferred view and the economic reality.

In the early days of the Kennedy administration, however, there was acceptance of the belief that the wage-price spiral should be held in check. The first meeting on economic policy was held in the Cabinet Room soon after the inauguration; it was one which I attended and in some measure pressed as to action, and it was largely devoted to this subject. In ensuing months the major industrial unions, especially those in automobiles and steel, were urged to moderate their demands – to keep their wage claims to what could be afforded from existing prices. Showing a cooperative spirit, the United Steelworkers Union, in April 1962, limited severely its wage claims in the then-current negotiations. This was to be a model for other unions. Immediately thereafter, however, the head of the United States Steel Corporation, Roger Blough, in one of the intellectually most deprived actions of the time, announced a substantial increase in steel prices and, in an amiable way, called on the President to tell him what he had done.

The Kennedy reaction was intense: 'My father always told me that all businessmen were sons-of-bitches, but I never believed it till now.'[2] Later, in a press conference, he thoughtfully confined the parental condemnation to steel men.

Under heavy pressure and diverse threats of antitrust action, tax audits and other reprisal, and because smaller steel firms wisely did not go along, U.S. Steel rescinded the price increase. For a time thereafter the controlling principle seemed clear: to prevent inflation at a high level of employment and output there must be wage and price restraint. What was generally assumed in European and Japanese wage and price setting was now establishing a somewhat fugitive position in American government policy.

Evident, unfortunately, was the enormously complex, tedious and controversial nature of any practical attempt to achieve this restraint, with the time-consuming, often frustrating negotiations involved. When economists compared this with the far more dignified sovereignty of fiscal and monetary action – something approaching a gutter brawl versus detached, contemplative macroeconomic decision-making – they were not unaffected. Macroeconomic policy moved to center stage.

The policy in the Kennedy years was openly, unapologet-

2. Quoted in Arthur M. Schlesinger, Jr., *A Thousand Days* (Boston: Houghton Mifflin, 1965), p. 635.

ically Keynesian. There must be a flow of aggregate demand sufficient to maintain the closest possible approach to full employment. The latter set the limits on what the economy could produce. Productivity – production per worker – was not a central issue. The educational levels of the work force, the supply and quality of capital plant, the role of technology and technological advance, had separate lives of their own. They were not the major subjects of concern.

As the Kennedy years passed, the basic design for economic policy became clear. Microeconomic or market restraint on wages and prices would have relevance but would recede in emphasis while, as indicated, macroeconomic policy would become the major focus. In these years the independently asserted role of monetary policy within the macroeconomic framework would also diminish. The head of the Federal Reserve Board, William McChesney Martin, Jr., was to prove amenable. After firmly asserting at White House meetings the statutory independence of the Federal Reserve and the role of its controlling board members, he yielded to pressure to keep interest rates stable and comparatively low. As the active instrument of policy, there thus remained only taxation and public expenditure – fiscal policy.

In 1961, the economy improved; there was still, however, the problem of ensuring what was thought to be an optimal rate of economic growth, a prospect to which the President and his advisers were strongly committed. Nothing would so serve social tranquillity, political success and presidential reelection as a population that could survey its economic position and find solid improvement over earlier years. A specific goal was set: the economy should expand its aggregate production of goods and services by 5 percent each year. Monetary policy having been set aside, affirmative government action called for either government spending to press the economy toward growth and full employment or tax reduction to release more income to private expenditure, thus achieving the same end. In minor, mostly rhetorical support of this latter course was the belief that it would also release more entrepreneurial and managerial energy to the production of goods and services, energy that the high marginal rates of the income tax were presumably restraining.

Beginning in 1962, there came the sharpest debate on economic policy of the time, and it led to a decision with enduring effect. That decision was to stimulate the economy by cutting taxes. Tax revenues were growing more rapidly than expenditures; let taxes be reduced.

The alternative to a stimulative tax cut was larger social spending, social needs being, as ever, evident and pressing, especially for the poorest of the people. Tax reduction, by contrast, was a conservative design, and it became one on which future conservatives would happily seize.

It is not surprising, perhaps, that my voice was firmly in opposition, but it was weakened more than slightly by being heard, at least in part, from distant India. I was not, however, wholly ineffectual.[3] It was possible to hold off final decision for some time, which I did with the support of Treasury

---

3. The proponents of the tax cut, at least so I was later told, were disposed to avoid scheduling key meetings on the matter when I might be back in Washington. Arrangements were made with the State Department to warn of any impending Galbraith return. It was called the GEW Line – the Galbraith Early Warning System.

189

Secretary Douglas Dillon, who reacted against any tax cut with more orthodox conservative reasoning. He wanted the tax system reformed; he did not believe taxes should be cut until the budget was fully in balance.

The outcome, however, was never seriously in doubt, and especially not after the Secretary of the Treasury was brought into line. The decision was firm by the time of the President's assassination on November 22, 1963, and the tax cut was put into effect the following year.

It was a watershed in American economic policy. Previously, when government support to the economy – to aggregate demand – seemed in order, thought and action turned, as during the New Deal years, to public expenditure. Henceforth they would turn influentially to tax reduction as a stimulative force. In the 1980s, the Kennedy tax reduction would be seen as the precedent for the Reagan action on taxes, including the extravagant reward to the affluent.

There were other important economic initiatives in the Kennedy years. One, led by Undersecretary of State George Ball, was for further liberalization of international trade. This also encompassed support of European economic and political union. These steps were on a broad current of history, the several factors making for a closer association between countries in the advanced industrial world. As regards trade matters, they were subject, however, to the peculiar rhetoric of the subject. Always, *ex ante*, the results of trade negotiations are avidly discussed and held to be decisively important; *ex post*, the changes disappear from sight. That is because the trade negotiations are normally small waves on the larger tide.

*

There was also in these years the new and vigorously asserted program to help the poor countries of which I have already spoken. The opportunity to participate therein was what took me to India. The Alliance for Progress, which was a helping voice in Latin America, and an explicit recognition of the role of the new African states on the world scene were also central in the thinking and action of the new administration. The concern was, alas, greater than the result.

A distinction must here be made between government action that is symbolic and that which is real. Thus, not the least celebrated international initiative of the Kennedy years was the deployment of the Peace Corps. The dispatch of eager and accomplished young men and women to render varied service from language teaching to veterinary medicine in the poor countries was both well publicized and well received. To those sent and to those helped, it was of no slight benefit. Of particular importance was the impression it gave to the world of President Kennedy, his administration and the United States.

However, the number actually involved in and informed by this experience in relation to the American youth population as a whole was infinitesimally small, as was the percentage of the poor people of the world so aided or so served. The Peace Corps (as also the Alliance for Progress) was rich in symbolism but of limited effect in relation to the enormous and intractable problems addressed.

In the Kennedy years, there was, however, the beginning of a domestic action that was to have large economic importance but that has only rarely been so recognized. That was the civil rights movement, and it calls for a special word.

191

In the long course of economic history, as I have sufficiently emphasized, few forces have so successfully resisted economic development as feudalism – the holding of the population or a large section of it in isolation in the service of rural landlords. This effectively denies to those so confined the sense of personal initiative and responsibility, the wider industrial opportunity and reward and the requisite education that are the hard substance of economic progress. They are, in essence, the prisoners of both the present and the past. So, in substantial measure, are their employers and masters. The imprisonment is greatly the more effective if the workers, because of race or color, are denied the chance for change that comes from the exercise of their political rights. The controlling point is clear: the American Civil War ended forthright slavery; it did not end the static feudal structure of the South.

By the 1960s, however, this system was breaking down. Economic change, brought on by the mechanization of agricultural production, that of cotton growing in particular, was releasing workers from their previous social and economic bondage. Many were making their way to the relative freedom of the industrial North. And now the civil rights movement – the drive for greater equality in educational opportunity, the attack on legally sustained segregation and discrimination, the demand for voting rights, the end to the self-centered political rule of the old landed class and its descendants – was opening the way to enlarged industrial opportunity and growth below the Mason-Dixon Line.

The movement also made visible for the first time a seemingly new and impoverished working class in the southern states and more especially in the large northern cities to which the former sharecroppers, in lesser measure, the onetime slave population, had escaped. When scattered over the countryside, with primitive housing, little education, sparse livelihood and no civil rights, the southern poor had been largely out of sight and mind, as are the rural under-privileged to this day. Now in the great urban areas they could not so easily be ignored. On this, more in the next chapter.

Meanwhile the point must be stressed: the civil rights movement was rightly celebrated for its humane and civiliz-ing effect. But it was also an economic revolution, one that is today taken for granted. In earlier times, the southern states had lagged greatly in economic development; that they would remain poor in relation to the rest of the Republic was assumed. Now no longer. Southern cities – Atlanta is a prominent case – show a strong and strengthening economic dynamic.

Economics is thought to concern itself with taxation, public expenditure, interest rates and the market system. Martin Luther King, Jr., is not remembered for his economic intui-tion or effect. In fact, one of the greatest and most evident contributions to economic advance in the Kennedy and subsequent Johnson years came from the second emancipa-tion, the consequent movement of blacks to larger economic and social participation and, most of all, from the decline and fall of the old self-serving feudal economic and political structure in the South. It is a lesson: in economic matters one must always look well beyond the proclaimed purpose of any given initiative to see its ultimate effect.

19

The War on Poverty
and the War

In 1965, when Lyndon Johnson took office after his election to a full term as President, there was an impression that the economic problems of the United States and therewith of the trading partners so deeply dependent on American well-being had been solved. The economy was expanding at a healthy rate; unemployment was at 5 percent of the labor force and declining. (As someone pointed out in those years, this should be read as saying that 95 percent had jobs.) Although prices were edging upward, there seemed to be no imminent prospect of serious inflation.

The wage-price spiral did remain a microeconomic threat, but intense and generally successful negotiations that year with and between management and labor seemed to keep this danger under control. In the latter days of the Kennedy administration a negative trend in the balance of payments had become apparent, with a resulting gold outflow. On special assignment from the President after returning from India, I wrote a paper expressing some alarm. Other economists in the administration saw the tendency as trifling. So, in later and better view, it was. The principal cause was the overseas economic revival and therewith the revival of exports which the United States had sought.

There remained the problem mentioned at the end of the last chapter – the very large number of Americans who, amidst this generally prosperous condition, were still abysmally poor. If they didn't find relief otherwise, it seemed possible that they would take violently to the streets, which they did in these years in several cities.

Poverty is not a central issue in the main current of economics and economic policy. The poor do not get many pages in the college textbooks or much attention in the scholarly journals. A minor change in interest rates or the public deficit is meat for major economic discussion; the continuing existence of urban or rural poverty is not. Here too economists reveal a strong impulse to avoid the more messy, intractable problems of their profession. In the dominant economic tradition there can be well-expressed sympathy for the deprived, but the policy and action needed to help them are not discussed in the mainstream.

Lyndon Johnson, more than John F. Kennedy, was sensitive to the concerns of the poor. They were something to which Kennedy had not personally been exposed; Johnson had seen them extensively at first hand in his youth.

In December 1963, a few weeks after President Kennedy's death, I sought in a speech in Washington to draw political attention to those who were not sharing in the general well-being of the time. Two or three paragraphs can perhaps be cited:

> On one elementary point there must be no doubt. If the head of a family is stranded deep on the Cumberland Plateau, or

if he never went to school, or if he has no useful skill, or if his health is broken, or if he succumbed as a youngster to [an urban] slum environment, or if opportunity is denied to him because he is a Negro [still the accepted usage], then he will be poor and his family will be poor, and that will be true no matter how opulent everyone else becomes.

Equally there must be no doubt that the means for rescuing this man or his children – investment to conserve and develop resources, assistance in relocation of workers, assistance to new industries, vastly improved education, training and retraining, medical and mental care, youth employment, counselling, urban recreational facilities, housing, slum abatement and the assurance of full civic equality – will require public effort and public funds. Poverty can be made to disappear. It won't be accomplished simply by stepping up the growth rate any more than it will be accomplished by incantation or ritualistic washing of the feet.

To the best of knowledge there is no place in the world where well-educated people are really poor. Why don't we select, beginning next year, the hundred lowest-income counties (or in the case of urban slums more limited areas of equal population) and designate them as special educational districts? They would then be equipped (or re-equipped) with a truly excellent and comprehensive school plant, including both primary and secondary schools, transportation and the best in recreational facilities. The construction employment in this part of the task would not be unwelcome. Then, in the manner of the Peace Corps, but with ample pay, an elite body of young teachers would be assembled – ready to serve in the most remote areas, tough enough and well-trained enough to take on the worst slums, proud to go to Harlan County or to Harlem.[1]

1. John Kenneth Galbraith, 'Wealth and Poverty,' speech given before the National Policy Committee on Pockets of Poverty, Washington, D.C., December 13, 1963.

Lyndon Johnson was favorably impressed by my views,[2] although, without doubt, there were other influences on his thinking, including, as noted, his own observations. One too easily claims originality or persuasiveness in such matters.

In late 1963, economists on the White House staff outlined a pilot program to test what might be possible as an attack on poverty; little so assuages the liberal and economic conscience at low cost as a pilot program. President Johnson discarded this proposal and suggested, instead, that $1 billion be committed to a serious effort to rescue the rural and urban poor. I joined a small staff working with Sargent Shriver at the Peace Corps headquarters, with the task of putting together a specific and detailed plan. Later, when the Office of Economic Opportunity was formally organized by legislative mandate, I was named to the supervisory board. My tenure came to an end when my opposition to the Vietnam war made me no longer an acceptable member, and Johnson withdrew my appointment. It was a metaphor of the conflict between domestic and military purposes. Of this, more presently.

The Poverty Program, as it came to be called, was a mélange: uncertainty as to what should or could be done was partly resolved by doing something of everything. Or, through the Community Action Programs, leaving the choice in part to the poor themselves by inviting them to organize and come forward with proposals for alleviating distress and ensuring escape from deprivation. The necessary funds – for education, including Head Start schooling for the very young and train-

2. See his memoir, *The Vantage Point: Perspectives of the Presidency, 1963–1969* (New York: Holt, Rinehart and Winston, 1971), p. 72.

ing in needed and basic economic skills, and for acquisition of community facilities – would come from the federal government. (In later practice, this flow of money would prove unduly attractive to local politicians, who would extensively replace the self-governing poor.[3])

The Poverty Program extended on to the Job Corps for training in elementary and basic work skills. There were yet other initiatives, including the Teachers Corps, proceeding, I believe, from my earlier proposal for the rescue of deprived schools and their children. All were worthy as to purpose and by no means unimportant as to accomplishment. Unhappily, the poverty remained.

Two factors of polar importance were responsible. The first was a deeply ingrained, even theological, opposition to providing income to the poor. The second was the prior claim of the military on attention and resources, including for the Vietnam misadventure. Rarely, if ever, have priorities been so visibly disarranged.

There is no more evident alternative to poverty than an income. Nothing, on the other hand, is so firmly accepted by most Americans as the damaging effect of money on the poor. We are at our most righteously compassionate in our concern for what unearned income will do to the unfortunate. And we perceive a practical danger as well as a moral one: the poor may prefer money from public sources to work, and that will cultivate a mood of dependence that will strike at the vital heart of the economic system.

3. See David Stoloff, 'The Short Unhappy History of Community Action Programs,' in *The Great Society Reader*, edited by Marvin E. Gettleman and David Mermelstein (New York: Vintage Books, 1967), pp. 231–39.

This danger is seen as peculiar to the underprivileged; for the affluent and the rich, idleness, called leisure, is not similarly deplored. On the contrary, the society is enhanced by having a leisure class. Those who are accomplished in the enjoyment of leisure are admired, not condemned; they have learned how to live the good life. They contribute as patrons to the artistic or literary distinction of the nation; they set examples of style and personal behavior, which are praised, even celebrated, for novelty, variety and extravagance. No one, or not many, criticize their indulgence.

The position of the poor is very different. Here, as noted, un-earned income is thought both morally and socially damaging, and so especially is the idleness that it may allow. This income and idleness are not forgiven even if it is clear that there is no employment opportunity available as an alternative. What is praised for the affluent is severely condemned for the poor.

The tendency of economics – and other social sciences – to adjust to the need and mood of the more fortunate, articulate and politically influential members of the community has been sufficiently noticed. It is powerfully evident here. There was much to be said for the Poverty Program of the 1960s – for its contribution to the Great Society, as that description came into use. Missing, however, was the guarantee that no American would be allowed to live in an intolerable state of poverty – that, as was the case in other industrial countries, there would be a reliable safety net below which no one would be allowed to fall.

The cost would not have been small, and some recipients would, indeed, have accepted such help as an alternative to better-paid employment. But neither the cost nor the moral damage would have rivaled the monetary cost and the grave psychic legacy of the military venture that brought the vision of a Great Society and, indeed, the presidency of Lyndon Johnson to an end. And success would have been a rewarding safeguard against the urban violence that is, as noted, in nearly inevitable association with economic deprivation.

There was no single factor leading to the now-admitted error of the Vietnam intervention and disaster. Military misguidance and mistake were amply present. In particular, the uniquely difficult problem of fighting a war in dense tropical jungle was not foreseen. In 1962, when I was sent to Vietnam on a fact-finding mission by President Kennedy, this was my strong impression from the military briefings. The limit on the effectiveness of air power that had already been so evident in World War II and in Korea was also not accepted. The military doctrine that if a country has air superiority, air warfare must be decisive was still unchallenged.

In the Cold War context and its frequent psychosis there was, as well, an exaggerated view of the unity of purpose of the Communist states – of the Soviet Union, China, Eastern Europe – and of their commitment to a Communist East Asia. From this came the deathless domino theory – metaphor controlling thought. Further, there was a grave underestimate of the extent to which any foreign intervention in Vietnam, however motivated, would be inextricably linked to the years of foreign rule – Chinese, Japanese, French – that had previously been experienced and endured in that country.

However, the most influential and unforgiving of all the errors was in economic and political judgment. Communism, comprehensive socialism, was thought to be not only possible but the wave of the future in the poorest countries, those with the most primitive administrative apparatus. In lands that had never experienced capitalism, Communism would, it was said, be a nearly irresistible force, one certainly that could be contained only by countering military strength.

That this view of Communism could be the basis of right-wing paranoia had long been established. Perhaps, considering the way passion invades thought, this was inevitable. However, the accepted economic or, more precisely, politico-economic view was broadly in support and agreement. No economic and political system ever enjoyed such awe and respect as did Communism in the mid-1960s. Let Vietnam fall to this compelling system and the rest of Southeast Asia would go. The threat would extend on to India, Pakistan and even Africa.

A relatively primitive country can with relatively elementary weapons fight a war, and especially in a jungle. There are centuries of experience on this. Modern economic life, in contrast, is far more sophisticated and complex. Communism could not succeed without qualified plant managers and trained workers, without industrial plants for that matter. In a primitive country it did not have and could not create the intricate public administrative apparatus that socialism requires. All this was ignored. So also were the objections of those of us reasonably experienced in the problems of the poor countries or otherwise disposed to raise questions. We were regarded with a mixture of suspicion as to judgment and forthright rejection as to conclusions.

A larger effect of the error of American intervention in Vietnam was that the military claimed both the political spirit and the financial resources that, plausibly, would have gone otherwise to the War on Poverty. And, a not unimportant point, those whose speech and energy would otherwise have been engaged in the latter were diverted to opposing the war in Vietnam.

A highly effective design for avoiding succor to the poor is to put forward the higher claims of war, defense, the military. There had been parallels before the Vietnam years. The First World War brought to an end the era of Woodrow Wilson, which gave the country the Federal Trade Commission, the Clayton Act and other elementary reforms. World War II took national attention away from the New Deal programs; in the words of Franklin D. Roosevelt, Dr. New Deal gave way to Dr. Win-the-War. The Korean war served similarly to restrain domestic reform, to label many reformers as agents of the Communist conspiracy and to warn many others against becoming so involved. The Vietnam war now did the same; and it would all happen again, if with no overt violence and death, with the arms buildup of the Reagan administration. The enduring legacy of that buildup would be the budget deficits that would effectively restrain future civilian social expenditures. It is by no means incidental that much military expenditure, that for sophisticated weaponry in particular, rewards a comfortably affluent part of the larger population. Far better that, it is held, than spending that impairs the character of the poor.

I participated actively in the 1968 presidential campaign as a supporter of Senator Eugene McCarthy, served as his floor manager at the Democratic convention and helped place his name in nomination. On that wonderfully contentious and in many ways decisive occasion, solutions for the problems of the poor – the Great Society – which had been so central to the discussion a few years earlier, received no attention whatever. The Vietnam war had erased them from liberal as well as conservative minds. In the social as opposed to the military dialectic, the triumph of the latter was complete.

In the 1972 election, the war now in decline, the problem of poverty was briefly restored to public debate by Senator George McGovern. As the Democratic candidate, he proposed a version of the negative income tax first urged by Professor Milton Friedman; this would have provided a basic underpinning of income for all Americans. It was defeated, and not least by attack from within the Democratic Party itself. Former Vice President Hubert Humphrey, subordinating his liberal credentials to political purpose, made it a major object of assault in the primaries. The proposal, which had once seemed highly plausible and which has its counterpart in other advanced industrial countries, was permanently buried. Welfare payments for the poor continued but as a conditional and dubious charity rather than as a social right.

Eventually the Vietnam war was brought to an end; American defeat, relatively undisguised, was accepted. By then the Great Society was long dead. And gone also was its founder, Lyndon Johnson. In this effort as also in his continuing and persuasive support of civil rights, going well beyond the Kennedy initiative and producing economic rewards that are now evident, he was one of the most socially perceptive and potentially effective of modern Presidents. Both he and his place in history were destroyed by a war that, it is now accepted, was the product of the most professionally accomplished of error.[4]

4. On this see Joseph A. Califano, Jr., *The Triumph and Tragedy of Lyndon Johnson: The White House Years* (New York: Simon and Schuster, 1991).

20

The Dim Years

The years from the end of World War II to the latter part of the 1960s are held by historians to have been a good time in the world economy or, more specifically, in the economy of the affluent industrial countries. As the last chapter told, there *was* the continuing problem of grievous inequality, especially in the United States, but, as also there told, this was not integral in established economic concern. In the 1970s, the benign view of the economic performance came to an end, along, not surprisingly, with the successful performance itself.

In the United States greater unemployment, relatively low economic growth and persistent inflation now became a fact of life. Into the language came the word 'stagflation' – a stagnant economy with substantial unemployment and painful price increases. Additionally, were one to fix upon the time when the decline of the United States on the world economic scene recognizably began, it would be in this same dim decade of the 1970s.

Four factors were at odds with American economic well-being. There was, first, the continuing pressure of wages on prices and prices on wages – the now-tedious wage-price spiral – and the reluctance of the more prestigious economics to deal effectively with it. The preferred instrument was clearly macroeconomic policy – tax, public-expenditure and especially monetary action – as against the politically messy direct involvement with wages and prices. Commitment to the latter, which became marginal in the late 1960s, would, with one major exception, be set aside in the 1970s.

Second, there was the highly specific matter of energy prices. Because of political and military disaster in the Middle East and the emergent power of the Organization of Petroleum Exporting Countries (OPEC), energy prices in constant dollars approximately tripled during the decade,[1] and this became an inflationary force in the economy as a whole.

Its effect was recognized, and more than amply so; reference to the 'oil shocks' became a prominent part of the discussion in these years. And for those who wished to shed personal responsibility for the poor performance of the American economy, the political convenience was compelling: it was more than agreeable to attribute the blame to the Arabs.

But this was not the only avenue of escape from responsibility. It was also held that inflation had achieved a damaging hold because of Lyndon Johnson's failure to tax adequately and in timely fashion for the Vietnam war. Inflation, in consequence, had been allowed to enter the system somewhat in the manner of a nasty virus infection. This was escapist nonsense but was widespread in its acceptance.

1. *Economic Report of the President* (Washington, D.C.: U.S. Government Printing Office, 1992), Table B-58, p. 364.

Third, there was also in the 1970s the beginning of a marked change in the public's attitude toward government, the federal government in particular. In the Kennedy and Johnson years Washington had been regarded as a strongly positive force in national well-being. When Richard Nixon took office in 1969, and especially after his reelection in 1972, it was his perverse genius to alter this perception, partly by words and partly by action.

The great Watergate scandal and the release therewith of a vast array of information on the more obscene processes of Nixon's government, including what was learned from the White House tapes, diminished confidence in the government generally. It now had the aspect not of an instrument for public betterment but of a commonplace and sometimes corrupt conspiracy against the public good. This attitude was confirmed in 1976, when Jimmy Carter was elected President after promising to rescue the country from the Washington political and bureaucratic establishment. The way was opened for the much more powerful attack on government that followed in the Reagan years.

Finally in the decade, there came clear evidence of the reduced competitive position of the United States in the world economy. Of this, more in the next chapter.

While the wage-price spiral as an inflationary force remained largely unnoticed in these years, there was one spectacular exception. Experiencing substantial price increases in the early years of his first term in office and facing a reelection campaign in 1972, Richard Nixon, with the support of his conservative economic advisers, did not hesitate. Although their commitment to the free market was eloquently avowed, their commitment to reelection was even stronger. Accordingly, in the summer of 1971, they forthrightly froze all prices and wages. This served well their immediate economic and political purpose: between 1971 and 1972, consumer prices were essentially stable. Then in 1973, the election having been won, the controls were promptly lifted. Economists in or close to the White House made no secret of their political motivation: once the election was decided, the free market could be restored. It was, by no small margin, one of the most cynically successful political actions of recent memory. For whatever reason, but perhaps because this made it clear that politics could dramatically overpower the reputable economics, this action has received relatively little attention in the far from sparse histories of Richard Nixon and his times. In the election campaign of 1972, George McGovern was, as we've seen, strenuously and effectively attacked for proposing a minimum income for the poor. There was little or no condemnation of Richard Nixon for setting aside the whole free market system.

In 1976, in the aftermath of the Watergate scandal, the dismissal for rather commonplace corruption of Vice President Spiro Agnew, the resignation of Richard Nixon to avoid impeachment and his pardon by his successor Gerald Ford, the Democrats were returned to the presidency. Prices had been rising steadily after their release from controls; production, the gross domestic product, had been essentially unchanged in real terms from 1973 to 1975. Along with the scandals, the meager performance of the economy no doubt contributed, at least marginally, to the Republican defeat. In the ensuing years, those of Jimmy Carter, everything got worse.

President Carter came to Washington with less of the intellectual baggage of economics than any of his predecessors at least since Dwight Eisenhower. He was thus almost uniquely open to the guidance of the professional economists who joined his staff. These were scholars of high professional standing who were fully committed to what had now become the post-Keynesian orthodoxy. To counter a strong upward push of prices from wage and price settlements, and specifically from the rise in energy prices, they continued to rely on tax and expenditure policy and additionally, and now especially, on monetary policy. Some empty gestures were made to wage and price stabilization – to wage-price guidelines, as they had come to be called. These were ineffective. Proposals for rationing the supply and thus controlling the domestic price of petroleum products, the natural answer to embargo and an external control of supply, were dismissed out of hand. Urging a simple gasoline rationing program at a meeting of economists at Camp David in the summer of 1979 near the peak of the oil-price crisis, I managed only to establish myself as mildly eccentric. Speaking that day at the same meeting, a distinguished economist from the Conference Board, one of the most influential of business organizations, confidently predicted a corrective recession for the summer and autumn of 1980. He did not note or even, one judged, reflect that this would coincide with the presidential campaign and election.

Consumer prices rose by 13.3 percent from December 1978 to December 1979, and by 12.4 percent the following year.

Monetary policy was accorded a strongly controlling role. The discount rate of the Federal Reserve, that at which it lends money to banks, was raised to 11 percent in 1979 and approached 12 percent in the election year following. Never had the Federal Reserve seemed so relevant and powerful. Unemployment, though moderate at 5.8 percent of the labor force in 1979, rose sharply the following year to 7.1 percent.[2] Carter, not surprisingly, was soundly defeated for reelection. The economists who guided him emerged with undisturbed reputations. They had shown that a good economist can stay reputably within the established parameters of economic policy, however disastrous the political result.

As President, Jimmy Carter was a man of decency and of compassionate instinct. On matters ranging from human rights to peace in the Middle East, his was a strongly positive influence, and his basic integrity and humanity have continued to be evident since he left office. He deserved a better fate from his advisers.

It has elsewhere been observed that much in economic life is made of the matter of mood. When the public mood is optimistic – upbeat, as it is usually said – people spend and business firms invest, and the result is a growing economy. When the mood is sour, glum, there is a severe constrictive effect on investment, production, employment and stock market prices. Consumer confidence is measured and the results are published to an attentive, solemn, even fearful audience. One consequence is that public officials at all levels,

2. *Economic Report of the President* (Washington, D.C.: U.S. Government Printing Office, 1982), p. 271.

high and low, are committed or compelled to affirmative comment on the economic prospect. Such comment has, by a wide margin, become the most common instrument of economic policy. It is not clear that it has any appreciable effect on economic performance, but that does not interfere with its use. During the long recession *cum* depression of the early 1990s, President George Bush provided an optimistic assessment of the economic outlook approximately once a week, but without any noticeably positive response. Perhaps, as was thought to be true of similar efforts by President Hoover in the early 1930s, there was a negative reaction: if things weren't bad and maybe getting worse, there would be no need for such frequent and fulsome optimism.

In this context, Jimmy Carter was a remarkable exception. When the economic prospect dimmed in the latter years of the 1970s and the last years of his presidency, he spoke plainly of the poor performance of the economy, making famous the phrase 'economic malaise.' Just as there is no proof that upbeat comments improve economic performance, so there is none that his words made it worse. They stand, nonetheless, as a memorable contribution to public candor. Not often and perhaps not ever has any President, when economic life has been unsatisfactory, similarly said so.

The economic policy of the latter 1970s had more than a domestic effect. There could have been no better design for weakening a nation's competitive position in the larger trading world outside. The Federal Reserve action has been noted. The prime rate of interest – that for the best borrowers – reached 12.5 percent and a little more in 1979 and averaged

15.3 percent in 1980.[3] The effect of such charges involves no mystery; it means that borrowing for economic purposes, for new or improved plant in particular, is impossibly expensive, thereby forcing obsolescence of machinery and equipment on the nation's industries. This came at a time when American industry was already encountering increased competition from more efficient foreign manufacturers. Through the early 1970s, there had been a fairly gradual increase in the dollar value of imports, the special case of petroleum products apart. Now, beginning in 1977, there was a strong upward thrust. Automobile imports rose greatly; numerous other imports rose exponentially. The United States, long the primary source of the industrial products it used and consumed, was no longer competitive in its own markets. And it was becoming increasingly less so. Among the new competitors were, somewhat dramatically, the countries that had been our enemies in World War II. Germany and Japan were now becoming powerful on the world economic scene, as was Italy. To the new industrial giants and the sources of their strength I turn in the next chapter. But first I must record a footnote on the American economic policy of the 1970s.

In this period and later in the Reagan years there developed the concept of government deregulation as public policy. The role of the state, it was held, had been too aggressively advanced; the market should be restored to its former eminence and authority, President Nixon's election needs apart. In the American experience this was to be a strong and especially damaging example of the error in substituting

3. There would be yet further large increases in the early Reagan years.

broad principle, verging as ever on theology, for relevant, if always painful, thought.

The consequences of this general resort to the controlling doctrine of deregulation as applied to banks, investment bankers and the now-infamous savings and loan associations will be detailed in a later chapter. Mention must here be made of its disastrously innovative application to the airline industry beginning in the late 1970s.

In the years following World War II, the United States had developed an orderly, competent and technically progressive air travel industry that was financially stable and reasonably economical as to fares. Fares and the allotment of routes were controlled by a public agency, the Civil Aeronautics Board.

This regulation was wholly consistent with established and sophisticated economic theory. Where, in the nature of an industry, a small number of firms compete – oligopoly, as it is known – there can be either a tacit setting of prices and services to maximize monopoly return or a disastrous price cutting caused by an erratic, uncontrolled competition. These were the obvious possibilities as regards the airline industry. Thus the need for regulation.

Nonetheless, another doctrine, more precisely a dogma, now intervened. It was that the market, however defective the competitive structure and, in consequence, however unpredictable or exploitive the expected behavior, is ultimately benign. With much fanfare, it was held that the airlines should be freed of government restraint as to both routes and fares. And so they were. It was a triumph of dogma over elementary good sense and even over the established economic theory.

Some immediate effects did seem favorable. New companies were formed by the optimistic and impressionable and entered the business; new routes were proclaimed; some fares were brought down. Quite possibly some new customers were introduced to the undoubted advantages of air travel. In a short time, however, the new carriers went broke or were absorbed; they and their investors were the first victims of the controlling doctrine. Soon older airlines were also in trouble.

Long-established companies – Eastern Airlines, Pan American – became hopelessly insolvent and eventually passed out of existence. Among those that remained, bankruptcy was endemic. Those escaping bankruptcy came to suffer heavy losses, and, in some cases, foreign carriers were looked to for financial rescue. The airlines so retrieved or otherwise surviving had as a primary hope that monopoly might eventually accord them a measure of stability. In the meantime, both routes and fares remained a shambles. Ticket costs on short journeys where there was no competition were exploitive. Longer-run fares where there were two or more carriers were unpredictably low. (As a broad rule, the greater the distance, the lower the price.) Needless to say, new investment in the airlines suffered; bankruptcy or the threat thereof has a clearly adverse effect on capital expenditure.

On one aspect of the industry the reform was restrained. Safety standards were still enforced by the government, even though this broke with the prevailing doctrine. The most committed ideologues are known to ride on airplanes, and they prefer on matters of safety to surrender authority to the state.

21

Victory from Defeat

The poor performance of the American economy in recent times has been more than amply discussed, as has the superior performance until, alas, these last years of the German and Japanese economies and, though less compulsively, the quite remarkable economic performance of the Italians. There are several reasons for both the imperfect record of the United States and that of the English-speaking countries in general and the success of their erstwhile adversaries. The tendency, even compulsion, to stress those factors that most agreeably accord with predilection is best countered by considering all of the causes of achievement.

In the beginning there is the matter of attitude and aspiration. The United States and its allies emerged from World War II victorious and dominant. Germany and Japan were in deeply somber defeat, and, if rather more casually, so was Italy. For the United States the evident, too evident, need was for continuation of success; for Germany and Japan it was for change and improvement: the psychology of contentment on the one hand, the power of aspiration on the other.

Further causes of the difference in economic performance,

however, go back to the last century and a bit before. One can even be precise as to at least one of the dates. For the English-speaking countries, the decisive year was 1776, when Adam Smith's *Wealth of Nations* was published in Britain. Reacting vigorously to the numerous trade restraints of the mercantilist era in which he lived, Smith left the English-speaking world with the durable impression that the state is the natural threat to economic life. So, indeed, was the erratically interventionist state of his time. After Smith, government and business in the English-speaking countries would continue to be viewed as inherently at odds; nothing could be so important for economic success as that business be free from the blighting effects of the state. To a marked degree, modern-day politics in Britain and the United States, in rhetoric but also in reality, revolves around this question. Those who speak to the need for relevant government intervention and those who avow the importance of leaving business alone to accomplish its inherently optimal purpose are in natural and vocal opposition.

A radically different tradition rules in Germany and Japan, especially in Japan. In both, paradoxically, it reflects the greater influence of Karl Marx and, in particular, of his deathless formulation that the state is the executive committee of the capitalist classes. What could be more natural, indeed more inevitable, than that it be in the service of the economy? It is to those who guide economic life, the business community, that the government systemically belongs. In Japan Marx is far better read in the universities than are the classical economists in descent from Smith. In Germany a strong historical tradition in economic, political and social thought derives also in some measure from Hegel and Marx, and it accords a dominant economic role to the state.

In practical terms, this means that the government must foresee the need for supporting investment in public works – what has come to be called, somewhat inelegantly, the infrastructure. And it must invest in the research and development that, because of cost or a too distant or too improbable return, is not profitable for the market-oriented business firm. An industrial policy, as it has come to be called, is assumed. And also a generally cooperative attitude between government and business.

The United States is not adamant in its opposition to such a policy; indeed, in particular cases, it was a pioneer. Beginning in the last century, large resources were committed by the government to agriculture; they were applied to diverse research and education, including the farm extension services. In more recent times, there has been the guarantee to the farmer of a return on investment by support to the prices of farm products.

The controlling reason for this intervention was not that the market system is defective in agriculture. On the contrary: the latter industry, as already noted, is the closest approach to the pure competitive model of classical and neoclassical economics still in existence. However, this model does not allow for costly research by the individual farmer. And market-price instability and associated risk, in the absence of government intervention, are a major bar to his investment in modern and expensive equipment or even soil nutrients.

The industrial policy as regards agriculture has been a striking success in the United States. Productivity gains in agriculture have, over the years, far exceeded those in industry. American agricultural products remain strongly competitive on world markets; farm labor requirements as a share of the gainfully employed have shrunk into near insignificance. However, when there is a discussion of industrial policy in general, little is made of the agricultural achievement. In the common economic view, as elsewhere noted, agriculture is a world unto itself; even those who make a case for the benefits of a government industrial policy only rarely bring it into their argument.

What is peculiar to agriculture in the United States is a commonplace for much industry in Japan and, if in lesser measure, in Germany. Governmental support, particularly through investment that has a longer-range and industrially more diffuse effect than would be possible from private outlays, has been of prime importance. This explains some, perhaps much, of the economic advantage enjoyed by these two economies.

However, in the United States there was one other, more intense application of industrial policy: in the arms industry. Here the effects, in contrast with those on agriculture or generally in Japan and Germany, have been not supportive but adverse.

Having suffered massive defeat in World War II, Germany and Japan were in no mood for either military adventure or military expenditure, both of which were, in any case, effectively forbidden them in the immediate aftermath. In the decades after the war, German military expenditures averaged around 3 percent of gross domestic product, those of Japan under 1 percent. American military expenditures, on the other hand, averaged 7.7 percent from 1952 through

1986. They were approximately 26.5 percent of all federal government expenditure. Back of these figures was a very different allocation of resources. What Germany and Japan had available for their peacetime industry – capital, manpower, industrial research and development, education, support to the infrastructure – the United States committed to its military establishment and especially to the development of increasingly exotic weaponry. By some estimates, as much as a third of all American engineering and scientific talent was so employed. This commitment was strongly continued during the arms buildup of the 1980s.

Such an allocation of money and talent to military purpose was not, it should be noted, the result, in any acceptable sense, of democratic decision. Leaving office in 1961, Dwight D. Eisenhower, in his most durable presidential comment, warned against the developing danger of a military-industrial complex, of a union of military and industrial power independent of the ordinary democratic authorizations and constraints of the political process. His admonition was more than justified. In succeeding years the armed services came to choose the weapons they would develop and deploy and the force levels they would achieve. Higher civilian authority was acquiescent or supportive; the civilian leadership of the Pentagon came to see its function and purpose not as exercising restraint but as supporting and defending the decisions of the military. The Congress, effectively influenced by military prestige and the specific interest in military expenditure and employment of the industrial firms so rewarded, supplied the requisite purchasing power. Liberals sought to show that they were practical, hard-headed and realistic by accepting military purpose and effective command.

If a public entity has control over the decisions as to what should be produced and what otherwise should be done and over the money to acquire what it needs, its authority is complete. Democracy with its inconvenient restraints is set aside. So it has been with the American military-industrial power.

From this kind of power the Germans and the Japanese were most conveniently free; their military establishments were politically and economically restricted, with the companion economic advantage just cited. Military expenditure, the great expansive force of the American economy in World War II, was now a strong restraining factor on longer-run American economic development. The Germans and the Japanese were the clear economic beneficiaries of their own defeat.

A further factor in the German and Japanese advantage can be found in the nature of the managerial dynamic in the modern corporation. This calls for a special word.

With age and an increasing scale of operations, it has long been observed, power in the corporation passes from the stockholders to the management. The board of directors, nominally the voice of the stockholders, becomes the passive instrument of the management that, indeed, selects it. Then, not surprisingly, since maximization of return is the avowed incentive in the market system, the management comes to pursue its own goals, to maximize its own return. This regularly takes precedence as the immediately relevant objective over the interest of the stockholders, the nominal owners, who are both powerless and unknown. That the individual in the market system so pursues self-interest the classically devout conservative must, in all faith, concede.

Responsible to itself, protective of its own position, the servant of its own interest, the management is interested in compensation, security of tenure and perquisites. Defending management interest in personal reward against hostile take-over attack and extending management power through merger or acquisition take precedence over efficient operation of the corporation.

When management attention is diverted from such efficient operation, the modern large corporation becomes subject to a bureaucratic stasis, an inner-directed bureaucratic immobility. Thought and needed change become subordinate to established policy. Initiative is diffused through the organ-ization and is tested not for its effect but for its conformity with what has been done before.

There is also a relentless tendency for the corporate bureaucracy to grow in numbers. Nothing is so agreeable as delegating the painful processes of thought or appointing subordinates to do the problem solving; thus the natural inclination of the management apparatus is, ineluctably, to enlarge itself.

The deadening tendencies here described are not peculiar to the United States, but it is the relevant case. American corporate enterprises are generally older, particularly as com-pared with those of Japan; the stultification process is there-fore further advanced. More important, in both Germany and Japan there is a close link between management and the financial and ownership interest; this is manifested through controlling banks, and management is held closely account-able, thus largely eliminating the tendency for it to sink into a self-serving mode. Present is the external power that is strongly interested in performance and earnings.

To these matters the accepted and reputable economics has been more than usually resistant. For some decades, going back, indeed, to 1967, I have sought to persuade that the separation of ownership from control in the modern great corporation has compelling significance for both theory and practical result.[1] The theory, as noted, centers on profit maximization; no other motivating force is so strong or, for that matter, is even recognized. Yet personal profit maximization by a management extensively empowered to pursue this end and the consequences have little standing in formal economic doctrine. Here, not exceptionally, that which is not easily accommodated to the approved economics is systemically ignored.

Finally favoring both Germany and Japan was the seriously misunderstood matter of labor supply.

There is no comment on Japanese industrial success that does not lay stress on a uniquely well-educated and willing labor force. When greater attention to American educational investment is urged, this Japanese advantage is always cited.

Education, basic linguistic and mathematical literacy, is not without importance. But for mass-production industry, as a wealth of highly visible evidence affirms, the most important qualification is the discipline and energy of those who, in contrast with earlier experience, find satisfaction and reward in urban industrial life. Those who do so prove to be willing and compliant workers.

---

1. See John Kenneth Galbraith, *The New Industrial State* (Boston: Houghton Mifflin, 1967; 4th edition, 1985).

Traditionally such a labor force has recently escaped from the greater oppressions of primitive rural existence. The point has previously been made: the individual who works as a peasant farmer is a harsh taskmaster for himself, as he is also for the members of his family. There may, as well, be the compelling exactions of a landlord. This is often a socially detached and lonely life. Better-paid factory employment, easier perhaps in physical effort and far superior in urban social situation, becomes immensely attractive. All these conditions combine to create the ideal industrial work force. The situation changes with succeeding generations. There is the greater appeal of other, physically less demanding, mentally and socially more rewarding opportunities. These generations desert the assembly lines and the work tables for what is deemed better employment. Those who remain demand wages and benefits well beyond the thought or aspiration of those who have recently emerged from rural poverty.

The sequence here described has been dramatically evident in the mass-production industries within the United States. Detroit is the highly visible case. Once its automobile assembly lines and body shops were staffed from the surrounding farms of Michigan and Ontario and more distantly from rural Poland and Eastern Europe. In the city of Detroit those so recruited found a hitherto unimagined reward. Their offspring, however, went on to physically and financially more attractive employment elsewhere. New waves of migration took their place, these, as noted, coming from the Appalachian plateau – the poor whites – and then from the Deep South. Detroit became a city of black population. No longer was there a low-wage labor force in the automobile plants; it would have been a much more costly one without the earlier migration, but the migration was now, in some measure, at an end.

In the years after World War II, German industry was staffed and powerfully sustained by eager workers from Turkey and Yugoslavia. (In other European countries — France, Switzerland, even in some degree Scandinavia — mass-production industry as well as other more tedious employments also depended on foreign recruits.) This work force was renewed as older workers returned home and others came in their place. Japan was at an earlier stage; during this time it had an abundance of willing workers from its own densely populated rural prefectures. Both Germany and Japan were thus admirably served by a refreshing labor supply, better served, it seems possible, than was the United States by its mainly internal migration.

It is not clear that this is an advantage for Germany and Japan that will continue. The presence of a large foreign population is now a source of social tension in Germany, although the hostility is directed more at recent political and often middle-class émigrés from Eastern Europe than at the established *Gastarbeiter* who work in the industrial establishments. The most interesting modern case, however, is Japan. It has exhausted its supply of local rural recruits and, because of insular position and ethnocentric commitment, it does not encourage legal immigration. Already there is much mention of a labor shortage there. Meanwhile other Pacific countries that still have such a reserve army in their peasantry -- Korea, Taiwan, Hong Kong, Thailand, Malaysia — are active in former Japanese markets. In Japan and perhaps also in Germany, an earlier industrial advantage as to labor supply may be coming to an end. That it has served well in past decades is not in doubt.

A word must now be said of another erstwhile, if notably unenthusiastic, wartime power, namely Italy. As have Germany and Japan, Italy has been a marked economic success in the years since World War II, with one of the highest growth rates in Europe and a standard of living that now challenges that of Britain.

No one has attributed this economic achievement to the precision of Italian government economic policy. Or to uniquely cooperative trade unions. Or, as regards the larger industrial firms, including the great government conglomerates — IRI, INI — to an especially qualified management. One must go elsewhere to seek the sources of the Italian success.

There are three. In Italy, as in the countries already mentioned, newly recruited and eager industrial workers have been available — in this case, former peasants from the rural south, the *Mezzogiorno*. This has greatly replenished the labor force of the industrial north and is now being supplemented by workers from North Africa. With the latter, it may be noted, comes what may now be regarded as the normal ethnic tension.

While suffering not less than other countries from the stolid and bureaucratic tendencies of management in its larger industries, Italy has also had a marked exfoliation of highly effective smaller enterprises, not a few of which function outside the official tax and regulatory economy. In Italy, perhaps more than in any other European country, there has, indeed, been a powerful rebirth of the much-celebrated entrepreneurial spirit.

Finally, and most important, there is the Italian artistic tradition. Drawing on this compelling inheritance, Italian consumer products have a marked advantage in design. And this illustrates a universal and insufficiently noticed dynamic: after consumer objects wear well and work well, they must look well – must appeal to the eye and to fashion. After the engineer comes the artist. Here is the true source of the Italian achievement: more than any other ethnicity, the Italians have recognized that the arts are not only enjoyable but, industrially speaking, highly functional.

This functional role of the arts, along with eager local workers and an increasing immigration from North Africa, has also been important in the modern industrial revival in Spain. There is a lesson here for the older industrial countries. Such high-cost centers of economic activity as New York, Paris and, needless to say, Hollywood also depend heavily, it should be recognized, on their artistic commitment. Without it they would be smaller, poorer or nonexistent.

In all economic attitudes there is an established view of economic life. It is of business enterprises with smoking chimneys producing goods for the masses. That such enterprises do go on to higher levels of technology is conceded. The factory, however, is the accepted end of economic achievement – of economic process and progress. That there is a further stage, in which design and entertainment are of central importance, commands little attention or respect. There is something casual or even frivolous about such a suggestion; the economy has to do with real production, real work. Here, as elsewhere, economics strongly, perhaps even proudly, affirms its own obsolescence.

*

In Japan, Germany and Italy past success has not assured stable continuing performance. All have now experienced a marked retreat from the optimism of the 1980s. In Italy governmental and corporate corruption has been shown to be diverse, sometimes imaginative and always extreme. Germany has encountered recession in combination with the problems associated with the merger of the two formerly separate states. In the worst case of all, Japan has suffered the abrupt end of one of the most notable speculative episodes of all time – in the common Japanese reference, the breaking of the great speculative bubble. Real estate values, securities markets, industrial markets have all had their day of reckoning, a classic case of euphoria and the always predictable aftermath. The longer-run effects are far from clear; the immediate consequences are exceptionally dismal.

This, however, runs ahead of the story; I return to the United States of the 1980s.

22

The Reagan Achievement

There have been few periods in American or world history, the years of Roosevelt and the New Deal possibly apart, that have been more scrupulously examined from an economic and social viewpoint than the 1980s. Much of the resulting judgment, though to be sure not all, has been unfavorable. Tax reduction oriented to the affluent, unduly enhanced defense expenditure and a large deficit in the federal budget were the prime manifestations of error. Related was a large and persistent deficit in the American balance-of-payments account, causing the United States to shift from being the world's largest creditor to being, by a wide margin, its largest debtor. There was erosion of the nation's competitive economic position, social tension in the big cities, financial speculation and manipulation extending on to widespread and unsubtle larceny and, in the end, the painful recession *cum* depression of the early 1990s. Eventually came the political reckoning: Mr. Reagan's party and his successor in office were thrown out of power.

It may well be said that the foregoing was and is the liberal view; that is correct, but there was, in fact, none other of similar influence. It is a view that seriously understates what the Reagan administration, given its purpose and that of its supporters, accomplished.

It cannot be claimed that Ronald Reagan and his subordinates had a consistently clear perception of economics or economic policy. However, any case that the 1980s saw an exercise in innocent economic error is badly misguided. These years saw, in fact, a largely deliberate and, in its own terms, successful economic policy. There was, to be sure, a social gloss over deeper purpose. This should mislead no one. The underlying purpose was clear, and, in very large measure, it was also accomplished.

The objective of the new administration coming to office in the new decade was, not surprisingly, to serve its own constituency. This was a well-defined community consisting of the comfortably rewarded in economic life extending on to the admittedly rich. They had come into being as the natural consequence of decades of generally improving economic well-being and, with the enhanced political voice and power accorded by money, were now a strong force in the American polity. It was this constituency that the new administration served. There were two well-recognized threats to its continued comfort, one domestic and real, one foreign and verging on religious belief, and both were addressed.

The domestic threat was the federal government, and specifically its power of taxation as this might be used on behalf of those outside the favored community. The poor in the Republic could be a costly burden; the progressive income tax could make a painful claim on the personal revenues of the affluent. In past times the government had made a commitment, sometimes real and sometimes rhetorical, to the welfare of the disadvantaged. In combination with the already substantial income tax, this commitment represented a decided danger to the well-being of the favored, or so it was perceived.

The deeper institutionalized or religious fear was of Communism. Communism overtly, deliberately destroyed and outlawed personally possessed wealth and income. At one time it had been thought a domestic possibility; for some it was still the ultimate danger from liberalism, the left. There was, however, the greater fear of the military power and prowess of the Soviet Union. This must be matched and exceeded. More immediately relevant, perhaps, was the fear that Communism might take over presumptively vulnerable countries in Latin America, Africa and Asia. This would pose a grave, if largely unspecified, threat to the United States, and, in any case, the people so endangered should be protected from this affliction. That is what the leader of the free world should do as a simple act of goodwill. Behind these threatening possibilities, committed to its earlier promise to aid wars of national liberation, was the Soviet Union.

From the experience of past taxation and the fear of more in the future to benefit the poor came, with remarkable consistency, the Reagan domestic program. The poor should, to the greatest extent possible, be removed from the public conscience. Taxation on their behalf should be placed under the heaviest possible ban. And present taxes should be reduced. There should be no hesitation as to relief in the upper income brackets.

Few efforts in American political history have been more

successful. Taxes *were* reduced, and in the decade of the 1980s any talk of tax increases came to be thought tantamount to political suicide by Democrats and Republicans alike.

Meanwhile, in response to the larger international fears, the Communist threat was vigorously addressed as a positive function of government. Since it was thought that the basic instrument against Communism was the armed forces, the military was built up in both numbers and weaponry to an unparalleled peacetime strength. More than incidentally, as I have noted earlier, the expenditure thus required also rewarded an already affluent part of the American citizenry. Such spending, however, was not believed to be justification for an increase in taxes – better to accept a substantial deficit in the public accounts. The deficit, in turn, became (as it remains) an independent force in its own right in keeping down social-welfare expenditures. These, unlike the military outlays, were held to be forcing the country inexorably into greater debt.

Two other lines of civilian expenditure remained sacrosanct. They were outlays for bailing out failed financial institutions, notably the savings and loan associations, and for maintaining the Social Security system – the provision or guarantee of old-age pensions. Both of them were in the service of an affluent or economically contented and also politically expressive part of the national community. Accordingly, they too were exempt from any effort at curtailment. Such expenditures were accorded an honorific role that eliminated concern for their effect on the deficit.

Looking thus at the Reagan economic policy and program as a whole, one cannot doubt its consistency as to form and purpose. A government committed to the interests of the affluent and the rich responded in a remarkably effective and comprehensive way. There were, however, certain symbolic and ceremonial constraints that had to be observed in connection with this broad thrust of policy.

Specifically, it is not thought acceptable in the United States – in the modern idiom, politically correct – to say openly of any action that its purpose is to favor the rich. There can be an expressed desire to do something for the middle class; on help to the rich there must be a decent silence. Nor can one be against help to the poor if it is for the avowed purpose of protecting one's own well-being. To be outspokenly hostile or even too obviously indifferent or uncompassionate is also socially incorrect and politically inappropriate. Accordingly, both policy for the rich and policy against the poor must have a covering doctrine. This cover need not be taken seriously; its role is widely recognized as verbal and symbolic. A disguise, however, can still be a disguise even though it is recognized as such.

For aid to the rich – the large reductions in marginal tax rates in 1981 – the Reagan cover was a declared need to stimulate more energy, initiative and investment. Effort by the already well-endowed was being inhibited because of the high marginal rates. It was held in the more extreme formulation that the energy released by tax reduction would lead to enhanced economic activity, increased public revenues, a reduced public deficit. This was the service rendered by the celebrated Laffer Curve, which held that beyond a certain point taxes reduced economic activity, income and tax return. It held further, on no empirical evidence, that the United States had passed that point; accordingly, lower taxes now would mean more revenue. Not everyone took Professor Arthur Laffer's curve seriously; this was not expected. Its service to the administration was as a disguise for the real purpose, namely to lower taxes on the affluent. Even an admittedly exiguous cloak over this intention was greatly preferable to none at all.

Complementing Professor Laffer was the well-celebrated work of Mr. George Gilder, *Wealth and Poverty*, which avowed that 'material progress is ineluctably elitist: it makes the rich richer and increases their numbers, exalting the few extraordinary men who can produce wealth over the democratic masses who consume it.'[1]

Similar and perhaps more successful was the position as regards help to the poor. Here income, indeed assistance in almost any form, was held to be damaging to character, initiative and effort and thus to the well-being of the impoverished. As the rich needed the incentive of more money, so the poor needed the incentive of less. As Professor Laffer and Mr. Gilder came forward to justify a greater return to the rich, the also distinguished Dr. Charles A. Murray came forward to justify in broad economic and social terms the excision of aid to the poor. The ideal course, he thought, would be to scrap 'the entire federal welfare and income-support structure for working-aged persons.'[2] Recognizing that this would be somewhat severe, he concluded that unemployment compensation might be kept and private charitable activity should be encouraged. There must be some suggestion of sympathy.

1. George Gilder, *Wealth and Poverty* (New York: Basic Books, 1981), p. 259.
2. Charles A. Murray, *Losing Ground: American Social Policy, 1950–1980* (New York: Basic Books, 1984), p. 227.

Mr. Gilder here added his well-heard voice: 'In order to succeed, the poor need most of all the spur of their poverty.'[3]

To these cloaks over deeper administration purpose President Reagan added, sometimes more vividly, his own. Government, he asserted, was not the answer to the social problem; it *was* the problem. Anecdotal evidence told of the futility of help to the poor. Some who seemed homeless really preferred sleeping outside on the warm street grates; it was their form of independent self-expression. He cited with no slight pleasure the case of a woman who was seen purchasing food for her family with food stamps after having invested her own evidently adequate resources in a bottle of vodka. Again the symbolic as opposed to the substantive cover.

There was a further and well-publicized service to his constituency by President Reagan and his economists. This involved the breaking of trade union power, bringing effectively to an end the microeconomic pressure of wages on prices, prices on wages, that had been so intractable a cause of inflation in preceding years.

In part, this effort was direct and forthright. In the early months of the new administration the air traffic controllers in the major airports went on strike. Theirs was a highly visible and indubitably important service. The new administration moved swiftly to replace the striking workers, punishing them explicitly with unemployment and at the same time vowing to keep the airplanes flying. This it did with marked success. It was an impressive demonstration as to how trade union power, thought by many to be nearly impregnable,

3. Gilder, *Wealth and Poverty*, p. 118.

could, in fact, be contained and broken. The lesson was clear for other employers and for the unions as well.

More general in its effect was what the new administration did as to monetary policy. The latter, which was already restrictive in the Carter years, was tightened rigorously in 1981 and 1982. Interest rates were sharply increased; bank borrowing was sharply reduced. In 1982, aggregate production – gross domestic product – fell dramatically, and unemployment as dramatically increased. Here the effective role of monetary policy, the pulling on that string.

This may not have been a wholly intended result. The administration had been briefly captured by what was to be the high moment of monetarism: the thought emanating from Professor Milton Friedman that prices would be stable and all would be well in the economy if the money supply, as it proceeded from bank lending and the resulting deposit creation, could be stoutly controlled. Repressive interest rates – tight money – that discouraged the borrowing and deposit creation would achieve this purpose.

Accomplished instead was the sharp recession, with Professor Friedman's optimistic design receding into the wings. There was a practical result of the recession, however, and that was a further strong check on union wage claims. This came as both union morale and effectiveness were weakened by unemployment, and employing enterprises were forced to resist wage increases in the interests of their own survival. It has never been sufficiently observed that strong trade unions require, above all, strong employers. Nothing so weakens a union's claims as the workers' need to keep the employer in existence.

The labor and monetary policy here conjoined went far

toward ending the wage-price spiral that had plagued macroeconomic policy in the previous years. The trade union movement, long a threat to an important part of the Reagan constituency, was also pushed back into the political shadows. So, as noted, were some of the employing corporations. The administration of Mr. Reagan was not above sacrificing some of its friends.

In economics the relation between a policy and its consequences is often sadly subjective. This was not the case in the Reagan years; cause and effect were in close and visible association.

As noted, the deficit that so effectively acted against social expenditure was not deemed adverse when incurred for military purposes. And the arms expenditure, in turn, had a strong sustaining effect on the economy. The result was a fairly solid rate of economic growth, ranging from 2.5 percent up to a high of 6.2 percent in 1983, and a reduced but still substantial level of unemployment.

President Reagan, given the supportive role of public expenditure, was the most clearly committed Keynesian since the Kennedy years, perhaps since John Maynard Keynes himself. Had Keynes still been alive, he would have been more than a little surprised by his latter-day disciples. He certainly would have pondered as to why policymakers who were so dedicated to deficit financing should seek, on frequent occasion, to separate themselves from his views. However, it is the practical action that counts; the stimulative effect of government expenditure in these years is not in doubt.

That there might be long-run effects, a time when the

accumulation of public debt and its associated interest cost would be a problem, was not seriously considered. It was a principal tenet of Reagan policy that, with any reasonable luck, the long run in this, as in many other matters – a prominent case being threats to the environment – would not come. During the eight years of Mr. Reagan's tenure in office, it did not. Again thought or accident had produced the sought-for result.

The striking achievement of the Reagan policies, however, was the improvement he made in the fortunes of the affluent and the rich while visiting neglect upon the poor. Here the results are beyond question. No one will ever have any reasonable doubt that Mr. Reagan did keep faith with his constituency.

Eventually the long run did, of course, come, and George Bush was the unfortunate legatee of the Reagan years. It would not be a happy inheritance. Before coming to this, however, it is necessary to take note of a highly significant development in the larger economic and political world. That was the collapse of Communism in the Soviet Union and Eastern Europe and the reassertion in those countries of the ethnic and economic identities of their citizens.

23

The Great Implosion

In the western or nonsocialist world the 1980s were, as we've just seen, a time of accumulating problems, problems that would become serious and painful in the following decade. To these I will turn in the next chapter. They are, however, but minor matters when compared with the upheaval, both incredible and unpredicted, that was taking place in Eastern Europe and the Soviet Union at the same time.

My interest in and attention to the economic and political life of that part of the world had been engaged ever since 1959 and the pioneering journey I have already described to visit and talk with fellow economists in the universities and research institutes of the Soviet Union. On several later occasions I returned, including once to receive an honorary degree at the University of Moscow. With a distinguished Soviet economist, Stanislav Menshikov, I wrote a monograph on the economic problems of the two systems.[1] None of this, however, prepared me for the dramatic nature of what

1. John Kenneth Galbraith and Stanislav Menshikov, *Capitalism, Communism and Coexistence: From a Bitter Past to a Better Prospect* (Boston: Houghton Mifflin, 1988).

eventually would occur. It was not until the early autumn of 1989, when, somewhat to my surprise, I was invited to lecture in Leipzig and Budapest, that I sensed, however slightly, that, in Eastern Europe at least, things were weakening a bit. A distinguished professor in the then German Democratic Republic and my host in Leipzig said, in commenting on the departure of students for the Federal Republic, 'You will still have quite an adequate audience.'

Any claim that one truly foresaw this enormous development would be seriously suspect. The extensive and highly sophisticated intelligence effort that sought knowledge of activities behind the Iron Curtain was supremely irrelevant. No word came on what might happen. The millions so invested brought no return. Not the least remarkable feature of this latter-day revolution was how completely it was not foreseen.

There were two reasons for this failure. First, there was the ambiguity of attitude in the western world toward Communism, including its particular manifestation in the Soviet Union. On the one hand, there was the common belief and assertion that it was a poor economic system, certainly far inferior to capitalism. On the other, there was the fear that because of its inherent power and appeal it might eventually attract, engulf and dominate the world. It was this latter possibility that strongly supported the military and clandestine effort and much intellectual vested interest. Communism thus remained in the minds of its adversaries both unsuccessful and dangerously successful.

Second, there was a nearly total inability to understand those forces making for revolution that are the counterpart of economic development and that were active in the Communist world. Each of these matters requires a special word.

The Soviet economic system and that of the Eastern European acolytes were, indeed, both strong and weak. The basic error in analyzing them was in generalization. Here I must repeat some points already urged. Their strength, especially in the Soviet Union, was in basic or heavy industry: steel, petroleum, electricity, transport, chemicals and, needless to say, armaments. In the more than forty years since World War II, the Soviet Union had established itself as an industrial and military power second only to the United States. There were now two superpowers in the world, and the Soviet Union was assuredly one of them. That was no slight achievement.

For heavy industry and armaments, the Soviet command and control system worked with obvious efficiency, a matter already stressed. The orders went out from Moscow; supplies and components were allocated; finished products appeared and were used. Industrial planning served well, and from this emerged the economic development within the Soviet Union that was visible to the rest of the world. From this also came, quite plausibly, some of the apprehension on the part of those outside. Widely overlooked were those areas of inadequacy and failure that remained and how they affected public attitudes within the country.

The principal failures, to remind, were in meeting the needs of the Soviet consumer and in agriculture. The successful consumer economy produces or requires a disconcerting number of goods and services. The goods are not only numerous but varied as to nature, style and design and unstable as to demand. The required services are varied as to training and preparation and unstable as to use. The Communist central planning system that worked adequately for steel, chemicals, tanks and nuclear weaponry did not work for consumer goods; it was too rigid and unyielding, incapable of accommodating to variety and change. Thus the inadequacy of the resulting products and services – clothing, house furnishings, restaurants, repair work, entertainment, much else.

Because consumer goods have, in the popular view, a light, even frivolous, aspect as compared with the products of heavy industry, and because the people of the Soviet Union did have the basic essentials of life, the shortcomings in the supply of consumer products were not taken seriously in much of the western discussion of the Soviet economic system. The commitment of a modern population to the consumer-goods economy was greatly underestimated. This was a serious error. Frivolous or not, varied, workable, well-styled and abundant consumer products and the companion services are what people want.

These attitudes were reinforced by the clearly evident ability of the western capitalist economies to supply both goods and services in comparative abundance. Television, the press and relentlessly improved communications told extensively of this success. The modern standard of living, to repeat, has far deeper roots in the public psyche than is commonly imagined. Westerners looking at the obvious extravagances and frequent inanities of their own way of life did not appreciate the urgency with which it was desired in Eastern Europe and the Soviet Union.

*

In the Soviet Union there was also the more explicit failure in agriculture, and this too was poorly understood. As hitherto observed, agriculture has traditionally worked well as an economic enterprise only when its workers and their families are subject to effective exploitation by themselves. The larger culture has reinforced these attitudes toward work. In industry, specified hours and reasonably agreeable working conditions have long been considered necessary; in farming, by contrast, the virtue of hard effort from dawn to dusk has been assumed. The individual who so committed himself and also his wife, family and hired man was a *good* farmer.

The Soviet Union abolished this exploitation and substituted the more leisured, socially more companionable and, some might even say, more civilized working conditions of the state and collective farm. This more relaxed life, combined with continuing and serious unsolved difficulties in supplying fertilizer, machinery and machine parts and in getting farm products efficiently to market, converted Russia, once called the breadbasket of Europe, into a permanent and large-scale importer of food grains. Widespread inadequacy in the agricultural sector become socialism's other failure, along with the scarcity of consumer goods. Only the private plots and the private farmers' markets, where individual responsibility and personal and family exploitation were preserved, were successful producers, and they accounted for a greatly disproportionate share of total marketed production.

As earlier noted, however, in the modern economic world agriculture with its problems is outside general economic comprehension. Agriculture, as ever, is for agricultural specialists; its economics is for agricultural economists. The failure of Soviet agriculture was amply evident and the subject of much comment, but the deeper reasons for its failure received relatively little mention.

The second and, in some respects, decisive factor contributing to the collapse of Communism lay in the field of, as it has come to be called, human rights. Here, too, there has been grave misapprehension.

In the modern industrial world, human rights – freedom of expression, security of person, participation in the decisions and processes of government – are widely regarded as an end in themselves. They are what the good and civilized society offers. They are the equal obligation of all governments and are equally possible for all. It is true that some governments are adverse, recalcitrant, oppressive; that is the way things are. Economic development, it is held, has little to do with the granting or denial of human rights.

In fact, above a certain level of economic achievement, human rights become not only a right but an inevitability. They are the product, or at least extensively the product, not of original virtue but of inescapable need. Nowhere does economic determinism, the controlling role of economics in human affairs, work more relentlessly and with so little recognition.

The controlling circumstance is far from subtle. By its nature, economic advance produces more educated men and women than, as a practical matter, can be kept quiet and excluded from a role in public life. Writers and poets; artists; scientists and engineers; journalists and television commentators; university professors and especially their students; lawyers, physicians and other professionals; industrial managers; labor leaders and self-anointed and aspiring statesmen

– all are brought into existence and supported by economic development. They are what economic development both needs and provides. Once present and numerous, they cannot, as a wholly practical matter, be denied voice. Nor can they be excluded from decisions on national affairs. They must be permitted to speak and to participate. This is the only solution; public expression and public participation must be allowed.

So, without exception, it has been in all countries as they have developed economically. So it was in recent times in Spain, Portugal, Greece, South Korea, Taiwan and, in substantial measure, in Thailand and Malaysia. And so it was, and predictably, in the Soviet Union and in Eastern Europe. Present therein were more educationally, professionally or artistically qualified people with more interests and ideas than could any longer be kept in silence and excluded from participation in government. Repression, as earlier observed, is possible in poor peasant lands and those with little or primitive industrialization. There the daily struggle for survival outweighs the urge for expression, and dictatorship is a practical possibility. With economic development that is the case no longer.

Communism sought to combine economic development, substantial if imperfect, with oppression, and this combination could not exist. Strongly adverse economic factors under capitalism can likewise, it should be noted, produce and cultivate repression, totalitarianism. That was seen clearly in Italy and Germany in the decades following World War I, leading on to Mussolini and Hitler. The danger may be present, as this is written, in the economic disorder of postrevolutionary Russia. This only affirms the point: economic success is a basic underpinning of human rights.

It is remarkable that the great revolution of the 1980s and 1990s in the Soviet Union and Eastern Europe involved almost no loss of life. The revolution of 1917 was an exceptionally bloody exercise; by contrast, the later one was almost totally peaceful. The deaths that did occur were caused not by the transition from Communism to an alternative economic system; they were the result of national, ethnic or religious conflict among people who were now endowed with the right of self-expression. These forces, and not the movement away from Communism, were the focus of disorder.

Economic development is commonly seen in material terms; it is thought to provide people with the necessities and amenities of life. In reality and more importantly, it provides life itself with some measure of security. The Russia of 1917 was a poor country; being poor, the people could be persuaded to slaughter each other with determination. By 1989 and the months following, Soviet economic progress, however imperfect, had, at least for the time, largely outlawed such behavior and such horror for those at risk.

The history of the second great Russian Revolution is not complete as this is written. Nor is that of the other countries that once composed the Soviet Union. It will not, one can already say, be celebrated as a compelling exercise in human intelligence. This was a transition that demanded restraint, careful analysis and, above all, thought. In the place of these, there was action according to metaphor and doctrine.

The hope was that sudden dramatic change – shock therapy

– would bring the magic transformation to capitalism. A brief period of pain, and the new system would be successfully in place. Many, including a sizable number of western advisers, believed that this should not be the mixed economy of Western Europe, the United States and elsewhere in the developed world but rather the idealized capitalism of free enterprise, of Friedrich von Hayek, Ludwig von Mises and Milton Friedman. Ideologically motivated scholars from the West found allies in enthusiastic new converts in the East.

This would not have been my design or my goal; when meeting with European socialists in Brussels in 1990 and on less formal occasions, I urged strongly against it. So mammoth a change, I contended, should be guided by thought, not doctrine. First to be redeemed and returned to the market should be the smaller consumer-goods industries, the services and, as possible, agriculture, all of which worked poorly under socialism. Here a cadre of willing entrepreneurs, many already in charge, stood ready to take over. The large industries should be returned more gradually to the market only *after* alternative forms of ownership and guidance had been devised. Meanwhile there should be control of rents, restraint of basic living costs, a solid effort to minimize the suffering from the transition. Above all, there should be powerful international help made available from the erstwhile and now-redundant military expenditure of the Cold War.

This was not to be. What has been proposed and what has occurred could scarcely have been a better design for giving both capitalism and democracy a bad name. The great anti-Communist revolt did lift from the world the terrible threat implicit in the opposing systems of the Cold War. But there is a darker side yet to be experienced and told.

24

The Uncertain Miracle

The beginning of the 1990s was dominated, not surprisingly, by the revolution in the Soviet Union and Eastern Europe. An imperfect economic system had come apart and, in some sense, was being replaced by no system at all. The controlling fact, however, seemed evident: Communism had failed – and where it did survive, as in China, it was undergoing major transformation. Capitalism, the market system, was triumphant. There was no lack of speeches to this effect; nothing so nurtures oratory as the commonplace.

The oratory in this case was, however, more than normally overdone. Capitalism, especially as manifested in the United States but also in Western Europe and Japan, was, as we have seen, encountering difficulties as well. There was, with much else, the enduring recession.

To say that a recession endures is to speak in contradictory terms. A recession is thought to be a temporary departure from the norm – from the substantially full employment of willing workers and a steady expansion in economic product. This has not been the recent case as this is written.

Beginning in the summer of 1990 in the United States,

there was depressed economic performance and high unemployment, ranging up to more than 7 percent of the labor force plus the many more who had given up the search for work and were no longer recorded. Economic stagnation and a high rate of unemployment continued over the next many months and acquired an aspect of permanence. The recession spread out to Western Europe and Japan. I have spent a not inconsiderable part of my life before congressional committees. Now, with the recession, the calls came again. What were its causes? What its remedy? I did not yield to the belief that if the economy were left to itself, all would soon be well.

It was a significant contribution of John Maynard Keynes to economic thought to suggest that the modern economy might well enter upon an equilibrium of underemployment and low performance. This was the living fact of the Great Depression. Now, in surveying the world scene sixty years later, one could see the reward of history: it was obvious that what had happened before might be happening again.

As noted, the accepted economic norm is high employment, a rewarding rate of economic growth. To speak of any other tendency is egregiously pessimistic. Perhaps it is also economically damaging. Politicians and even scholars should show confidence; the economy should be viewed affirmatively by all responsible people. Economic pessimism (and nothing could be more pessimistic than the idea of an underemployment equilibrium) destroys confidence and inhibits consumer demand and industrial investment. It is, in an innocent way, subversive. Nonetheless, by 1993 as this is written, when a 'recession' has lasted three years and more, the possibility of a depressive equilibrium as regards unemployment can no longer be ignored. There is need, however, to distinguish between causes that are obviously temporary and those that are possibly permanent.

There were economic legacies from the 1980s that, by their nature, were temporary in effect; while both precipitating and deepening recession, they would, with the passing of time, release the economy from their depressive influence. Thus the decade was a period of massive speculation in the financial markets, and especially in real estate. The Florida real property boom of the 1920s reappeared in nearly all the major cities of the nation, with the banks, small, large and very large, joining in to finance it. After the collapse of this speculation, as all speculative episodes do collapse, there remained the economic wreckage – empty office buildings, an idled construction industry, banks replete with bad collateral and newly discovered executive error, a sharp restriction on new bank lending.

To the depressive effect from the banking system and the speculation there financed was added even more visibly that from the savings and loan associations, by abbreviation the infamous S&Ls. These, like the airlines, had, in pursuit of guiding principle, been released from regulation some years earlier. But in a striking example of the differential social concern that allows social action, even socialism, if it is for the affluent, the S&Ls were allowed to retain a highly effective access to government funds through public guarantee of their deposits. So endowed, they went on an unparalleled speculative spree, which was laced with a far from subtle admixture of both mental delinquency and forthright larceny. Proposals for reinstituting regulation were righteously rejected by Reagan administration officials.

The inevitable economic result of the ensuing collapse and scandal was not only diminished lending for new construction and home purchases but also a heavy market overhang of real estate belonging to the enterprises taken over by the government for liquidation.

With time, the depressive effect of the real estate speculation, the banking troubles and the S&L disaster will come to an end. A new confidence leading on to the next episode of speculative euphoria will arrive. So it has been; so it will be. Thus does time work its therapy.

Similarly subject to the remedial effects of time is the mergers-and-acquisitions, leveraged-buyout mania. This too was strongly but not permanently depressive.

It has sufficiently been stressed that in the modern large corporation authority resides in normal circumstances with the management. And all accepted economic doctrine assumes – and no doubt rightly – that the basic objective of the industrial firm is the maximization of return. The great mergers-and-acquisitions mania of the 1980s in its several designs was the result of the desire to protect and enhance the profit and also the prestige and power of the managers – the executives. Similarly, the leveraged buyouts defended the existing management from corporate raiders – from those who, in search of their own wealth and aggrandizement, threatened the executive position, prestige and return of those already in command. (It also provided a rich reward to the investment bankers and the lawyers who stimulated, financed or guided the process.)

The common result of both the mergers and acquisitions and the leveraged buyouts was the substitution of debt for equity. Money was borrowed to buy up the stock of firms being acquired or preventively to buy the stock that was in danger of giving control and therewith pay and prestige to hostile raiders. In both cases there could be a temporary monetary return to the selling stockholders; more durably, the newly merged firms and the firm bought out by its management were burdened with debt from the exercise. Servicing the debt, in turn, had a strongly depressive effect. Investment expenditures had to be curtailed, and particularly any with a longer-run reward, such as those for research and development. Unpromising units were sold or closed down. Payrolls were aggressively trimmed, adding to the already growing unemployment.

With time, these adverse effects also lose their force. The claims of debt diminish; new investment is encouraged; employment and income increase.

The junk-bond episode of the 1980s will have, perhaps has had, a similarly short aftermath. There was nothing remarkable about this aberration; simply said, it was discovered yet again that individuals and institutions flush with, or anyhow possessed of, cash would buy securities regardless of risk were the interest returns high enough. For junk bonds these returns were very high, ranging well upward from 15 percent; assuming there was no loss, this was very attractive. The possibility of loss was then ignored. Investment bankers, and particularly the then-much-admired house of Drexel Burnham Lambert, underwrote the bonds, which is to say they acquired them for sale to a largely unsuspecting public. When, as ever, the day of reckoning arrived, the junk market collapsed, and the less fortunate were left in possession of now-worthless paper. Drexel Burnham Lambert passed into bankruptcy; its most distinguished and highly rewarded operator, Mr. Michael Milken, passed into a minimum-security jail. For the economy as a whole there was a further depressive effect from those left newly impoverished, but this, too, like so much else, will be forgotten with time.

We have here the most direct and visible causes of the recession of the early 1990s, and in them lies the hope that it will prove to be a temporary phenomenon. The memory of the great speculative episode fades. The financial mind turns from the past to the next great premise.

More substantively, debts are liquidated by default or as bankruptcy proceedings take their course. Empty office buildings eventually gain inhabitants. Banks, their bad loans written off, lend again. All of this is part of established experience. It is largely what gives meaning to the concept of the business cycle. It is why the word 'recession' carries the connotation of a *temporary* departure from a better norm. As this is written, recovery from the long recession of the early 1990s is indeed a prospect.

However, as one views the aftermath of the 1980s and the conditions in the early 1990s, there is the less benign possibility. Perhaps the American economy and the world economy have entered a new phase in economic development; perhaps there is the previously mentioned tendency for the economy to find its equilibrium not at full employment but with a substantial level of unemployment, this despite a moderate rate of economic growth.

This possibility can be traced in part to the distribution of income. When viewed as a social concern, a reasonably equitable distribution of income is traditionally urged; it contributes to a sense of fairness and is a manifestation of social justice. Such a thought is, however, strongly condemned and righteously resisted by those of more conservative, politically cautious belief. For them it assails the principle that what one receives is either a human right or a needed incentive; it invades and sets aside one of the high principles of the market system.

Not mentioned in this continuing and often ardent debate is the possibility that a highly unequal distribution of income can be dysfunctional as regards the performance of the economic system. That may well have been the case in the United States in recent years.

Specifically, when income is equitably distributed, there is little question as to its ultimate disposition. It is spent or it is saved, invested and thus spent. There are no large pools of funds that are held in idleness because no one, or not many, have sufficient income to support such accumulations.

The United States in recent times has had both an unequal and an increasingly unequal distribution of income. Paul Krugman has estimated that in the 1980s '70 percent of the rise in average family income [went] to the top 1 percent of families. . . . The 1 percent of families with the highest incomes received about 12 percent of overall pretax income, while the wealthiest 1 percent of families had some 39 percent of net worth.'[1]

The counterpart of this concentration of income and wealth

1. Paul R. Krugman, 'The Right, the Rich and the Facts,' *The American Prospect*, Fall 1992, pp. 19–24.

is a damaging unreliability as to its use. In established and orthodox economics, savings are invested and spent no less reliably than the money that goes to the supermarket. In real life, if money goes to individuals in very large chunks, it may be neither spent nor invested. It may be held in liquid form; some of it, as in the 1980s, may be absorbed by functionless debt creation, such as that which financed the mergers and acquisitions and the leveraged buyouts.

With recession and its aftermath there is a further adverse effect on spending and real investment. Then, as the product of economic uncertainty, the urge to personal liquidity becomes stronger. Income is paid out; there is no companion return to consumer purchase or real investment. The poor spend what they receive in good times and bad. So, on the whole, do those with middle incomes. The rich have a choice. When they neither spend nor invest, a new equilibrium is set by the reduced demand. To keep the economy at full employment, there is then no alternative to a supporting government expenditure – the deficit.

This was the unintended history of the 1980s. Tax reduction returned income generously to the rich; so did speculation. To compensate for the income functionally so idled, the federal government ran deficits in a range from $128 billion to $221 billion. (Previously, under President Carter, the deficit had been between $40.2 billion and $79 billion.) Nothing more distinguished President Reagan from his predecessors than his commitment to deficit financing. Without this government support to the economy as an offset to idled, unspent income – a good part being governmental outlay for the defense buildup – economic growth would have been much lower and unemployment much higher. The recollection of the Reagan presidency would not have been of its seven fat years. The recession that followed on the collapse of the speculative boom of the 1980s would have been greatly more serious without this support.

None of this has been much discussed. There remains, to repeat, the deep public and professional economic commitment to the full- or high-employment norm. To this, it is believed, the economy will always return by itself. Often this is stated in metaphoric terms: 'The economy is fighting its way out of recession.' 'It is struggling to recover.' There is a companion resistance, equally strong, to seeing income distribution in functional terms – as a factor bearing on economic performance.

There is an undoubted problem in using the government deficit to sustain the flow of purchasing power – aggregate demand – and it is not especially subtle. If adequate, the government support so provided can work effectively in the short run; then the long run arrives. It becomes necessary to command more of the public revenue to service the national debt. That, an essentially sterile claim, takes precedence or seems to take precedence over socially more useful functions of the state.

Given the possible tendency for the modern economy, in the absence of state support, to find its equilibrium at inadequate levels of employment, the deeper causes must be discovered and therewith the relevant remedies. The distribution and resultant spending of income must come ineluctably to public attention. There is, as I've said, a social case for equitably distributed income, but the latter, to repeat, is also functionally necessary for the effective operation of the modern market economy. That the recession *cum* depression of the 1990s came first to the United States and spread out to the world from here should surprise no one; as to widely distributed and therefore reliably expended income – the first essential of modern capitalism – we are far from the best case.

When one looks at the present scene, a further possibility emerges, one that is also rarely mentioned in our time. It is that in the modern polity, continuing unemployment is preferred by many (and especially by those with political voice and influence) to more vigorous employment expansion and especially to the measures necessary to achieve it.

In the modern economy an influential part of the population is in a relatively secure position as to income and earnings. There is the large corporate bureaucracy. Much is made in poor times of those workers who are shed; there is little mention of the comfortable position of those who do the shedding. There is also the large public bureaucracy and the very extensive professional class: doctors, lawyers, academicians, accountants; the list goes on almost indefinitely. Here, too, unemployment is not deeply felt or feared; for many and perhaps most in these circumstances, professional position and pay are secure, and the stable living costs are not unwelcome.

There are also the large number living on Social Security or pensions, and they are either unaffected or favorably affected by unemployment or, for that matter, recession or stagnation. Inflation is then less of a threat to the many with fixed incomes. Unemployment is regretted but less so when suffered by others unknown. For numerous employers there is available with greater unemployment a more willing, more amenable, less assertive, more stable labor supply.

Underemployment is especially to be preferred to the measures that contend with it. Government expenditure on employment would add to the deficit, and from this could come the specter of future tax increases. Low interest rates, even if not especially effective against continuing unemployment, are adverse to rentier income. They also lower the price that banks charge for their salable product, namely the money they lend. Bank and central-bank influence, under the shadow of seeming neutrality, is usually against what is called 'easy money.' Longer-run steps to correct the adverse functional distribution of income clearly would be unwelcome to all so affected.

It is not possible in the world today to seem to be in favor of unemployment. So to argue openly would be thought profoundly eccentric. The fact remains, and with a powerful influence on public policy: for a substantial and very influential part of the modern industrial population, the underemployment equilibrium is not an adverse phenomenon and, to repeat, is much to be preferred to the relevant corrective action. This, too, is a shadow on the modern capitalist miracle.

25

The Last Chapter

I come to the end of this journey. As one surveys the contemporary scene, it is not all dark or even gray. The great confrontation extending over the globe between capitalism and Communism is in the past. One has only to reread the history of the Dulles and Kennedy years to realize from what danger the world has thus escaped and how many in the United States and certainly also in the Soviet Union owed their high positions to their sophisticated view of the several strategies for reciprocal and comprehensive annihilation.

Have we forgotten that during both the Eisenhower and Kennedy administrations people were being instructed on building bomb and fallout shelters, all for the apocalyptic day? Asked for my opinion by President Kennedy, I helped persuade him to veto a small illustrated publication telling how to dig a backyard shelter and picturing a nice American family escaping from the nuclear danger in their boat. Those who lived in three-story tenements or high-rise housing projects did not have such choice.

In the mid-1990s, there is still the continuing and grave threat from impoverishment and political disorder in Eastern

Europe and the former Soviet Union in the aftermath of the revolution. This could endanger peace both there and in the larger world in the years to come. And peace in the poor countries of the planet is still as much an exception as the rule. This calls for a special word.

The contrast between the fortunate lands and those that are not is a dominant fact in the world today. It may become more pronounced, at least insofar as it has depended on aid from the rich to the poor. That aid in the past, especially from the United States, was, in part, a consequence of the Cold War. It was the product of a less than graceful alliance between the concerned and the paranoid – between those with a serious desire to help the needy and those who saw in such help a defense against the spread of Soviet influence and Communism.

Now no longer: this alliance has gone forever. Aid to the poor is now only a matter of concern and conscience. It invades the culture of contentment and invokes the risk of heavier taxation, a matter to be stressed in a moment.

A few fortunate lands already mentioned – Taiwan, Korea, Singapore, Thailand, Malaysia, Indonesia, in substantial measure China and in some measure India – have escaped the wholly desolate poverty of the past. For others, especially those in Africa, the prospect still ranges from grim to appalling. There must be pressure from people of goodwill to continue assistance, with, as earlier indicated, a special stress on education – human investment. Without the specter of Communism, it will not be easy.

At the same time there must be an end to one of the more disastrous legacies of the Cold War, namely the supply of arms to the poor countries and the arms trade in general.

Arming the poor nations as an instrument against Soviet power and Communism was always highly irrelevant. Now the irrelevance of arms aid is total. And it commands resources that are urgently needed for economic development and yet more as the alternative to starvation. The arms fuel the domestic conflicts that are gravely destructive of both people and economic and social progress.

On the latter there must, in the future, be a new view of the sovereign power of the individual nation, which up until now, and especially in the postcolonial era, has been thought sacred. As such, it has served as a shield for cruel and socially devastating internal conflicts, all undertaken as a sovereign right.

This cannot continue. There must be a suspension of sovereignty by international authority when this is necessary to stop domestic slaughter. This, needless to say, must be done through the United Nations; it is not the right or obligation of any one state, including the United States. In Somalia and in very tentative fashion in the Balkans, this international responsibility is already emerging as this is written. It must continue not as the exception but as the normal response to unspeakable domestic conflict. It is not the sovereign right of one country to attack another; no more is it the right of a country to destroy its own people.

Aid and international intervention to stop domestic hostility and slaughter notwithstanding, the contrast between the rich and the poor will still be stark.

I return to the more favored world.

Established capitalism, as it exists in Europe, the United States, the other English-speaking countries and the Pacific lands, is essentially a peaceful system. And so, barring the tensions that would surface from enduring economic depression, it will remain.

The modern advanced economy is peaceful partly because, as has been sufficiently noted, its more fortunate people have something to lose. The rich or the merely affluent, facing, along with the camel, the eye of that biblical needle, do not take readily to the risk from personal demise. The poor are more willing or have no choice. In the time of the Vietnam war the more fortunate youth in American universities were the focal point of resistance. Nor do they now show much enthusiasm for service in the armed forces. That, it is thought, is for the less favored, the minorities and the poor, a matter to which I have given a measure of attention.[1]

More generally, modern economic life crosses national boundaries to form a comprehensive and intricate association that is a powerful solvent for aggressive and regressive nationalism. Trade, investment, communications, travel and transnational corporations all so serve. From this comes the first of the dialectics of our time.

On the one hand, there is the broad thrust to closer economic and political union. This is evident in its most developed form in Europe in the EEC, the European Economic Community, with its somewhat elementary government in Brussels, but there are also the North American Free Trade

---

1. Especially in the ground forces, the representation from white upper-income communities is minimal. I was asked in 1991 by then-Congressman Les Aspin to testify on this subject before the House Armed Services Committee. My appearance was first postponed and then canceled. The Gulf war had arrived; the social and ethnic composition of the armed forces was not a matter that could then be discussed in a tactful way.

Agreement, or NAFTA, and a very preliminary movement as between the Pacific Asian countries and Australia.

Countering this trend is the social and economic role of the modern state. The provision of medical care, education, housing and much else and therewith the budget, taxation, macroeconomic policy and maintenance of employment levels are now the responsibility of the individual government. These efforts vary greatly in coverage, cost and competence and in manner of payment and larger fiscal effect, including budget deficits.

Thus the dialectic. On one side there is the strong political and economic appeal of the larger community – of Britain, France and Germany no longer in conflict but in close, harmonious, civilized and politically safe association with each other and with other European states. On the other are the social tasks and responsibilities of the individual nation and, as noted, the related and diverse macroeconomic performance as to budgets, taxes, expenditures and deficits. Also resisting the claims of the larger association is the ancient and enduring sense of national and language identity.

These are not matters that are readily surrendered to the more distant, perhaps more amorphous, government of the greater union. The conflict between the advocates of association and the advocates of separate states is currently creating intense debate and dissension in Europe. The sharpest focus is on the plan for a single currency. This is a very attractive goal but one that definitely must await coordination of the economic and social and therewith the fiscal policies of the individual states. Without such coordination, a common currency is a superficially compelling but idle dream.

Debate over NAFTA in the United States and Canada turned

in a much more elementary way on the extent to which domestic social concerns, especially employment, the environment and other national questions, should be sacrificed to a larger, politically civilized association, with obvious economic advantages for influential economic interests. This debate will not end with the favorable decision. The basic dialectic – the rights of individual sovereignty against the gains from closer union – will, in one form or another, continue.

The second and deeper dialectic of this decade exists within the modern state. At one time there was the all-embracing and continuing struggle between capital and labor, employers and the working masses. Democracy was a thin disguise for this conflict; political voice was on one side or the other, and most frequently, one cannot doubt, on the side of the capitalists. Unacknowledged but ever present and accepted by all were the bearded face and long arm of Karl Marx. Capital and labor, capital versus labor; what else is there?

Now no longer. The capitalist has been swept into the great corporate bureaucracy. International competition has weakened what once were the evident powers of monopoly and oligopoly. Where once in the United States, Canada, Britain and other of the older industrial countries there was fear of corporate power, there is now deep concern for corporate incompetence and weakness. This has greatly changed the terms of what was once the class struggle.

I've made the point before. A strong working-class movement, strong unions in particular, require strong employers. When the latter weaken, so do the unions. No longer are there affluent earnings to seek and appropriate. Instead, there is worry about employer survival and, in the frequent case, a financial commitment by labor thereto. The class struggle has become a pale ghost of its past.

There is now instead a new and relevant dialectic, that between the large, economically and socially comfortable community that has come into being in the advanced economic society and those who live on the margins of the modern economy or outside.[2]

Those who now combine well-being with political power are the many, not the few. To the once powerful and still affluent financial and business community – managers and bureaucrats replacing the old-fashioned capitalists and still-surviving entrepreneurs – are added the large and wide-ranging professional, academic, cultural and entertainment community, the great modern rentier class and the vast numbers of the retired. Here are both political voice and votes. Here, as earlier noted, there is a measure of contentment even with a poorly performing economy. The discomforts of recession and an underemployment equilibrium are for others to suffer.

Outside are those who do the tedious work, staff the service industries, are involuntarily unemployed or have given up or rejected the search for employment. From within the well-to-do community there are undoubted and sincere expressions of concern for those outside. But it is the larger comfortable community that rules, and broadly and not surprisingly, it rules in its own interest. Modern politics, most visibly in the United States, is dominated by it, and partly for this reason many of those outside do not vote; there is no point in going

2. I have recently dealt with this in some detail in *The Culture of Contentment* (Boston: Houghton Mifflin, 1992).

to the polls if there is little to choose as between those aspiring to public office.

Social and political conflict is not now, and in the future will not be, between capital and labor; it will be between the comfortably endowed and the relatively or specifically deprived. This may not, perhaps will not, be peaceful. Political voice and participation are the solvent of tension; when these are not available, violence becomes the alternative. The danger is already evident in the United States. In Europe also the great voiceless underclass imported from abroad to do the physically exhausting and mentally enervating work of the modern economy is a source of fear among those who, on ethnic and other grounds, also resent its presence.

The steps needed to relieve tension or resolve conflict are not in doubt. The economy must be so managed and, as necessary, supported as to provide ample employment opportunity. This requires strong macroeconomic action – public investment and job creation – when that is needed to break the underemployment equilibrium. And it means budget restraint when the economy is functioning well.

For those to whom employment is not available and for those who cannot work, there must be a secure safety net to which there can be resort without social condemnation.

There must also be a strongly effective educational system; nothing is so important for the upward mobility that is a prime solvent for social tension. And it must be recognized that in no industrial country does the market system provide good or even habitable housing for lower-income tenantry. And there must be universally available medical care and counseling for drug and alcohol abuse.

There is no great debate as to these needs, or most of them;

there is a sense of the commonplace in citing them. But merely to list them is to see that all are, in substantial measure, at public cost. Thus the problem: rather than take on that cost, it is far easier for the comfortable to find flaws in the character of those who make up the underclass and increasingly also in the immigration laws and their enforcement. And to find social virtue in a seemingly principled resistance to taxation and the invasive state. And, as trouble looms, to call for more police and more stringent jail sentences or to move to the suburbs.

It is the nature of the comfortable community that it takes a protective, short-run view of its own position. It must be noted again that there is no substantive measure to relieve poverty or improve the lives and ensure the calming upward mobility of the underclass that does not require action by the state, although there is both oratory and seemingly sophisticated argument to the contrary. The purpose of the latter is not to produce results but to relieve those who are more privileged of adverse conscience and cost.

Here, as to economic life, is the present and the future. The future will turn on the outcome of the conflict between the social and economic autonomy of individual countries and the economic and political appeal of the larger community. And it will depend on the outcome of the quiet and perhaps not so quiet war between the comfortable and the underclass.

No one can now say how these matters will be resolved; those who so specify go beyond the range of serious fact and available knowledge. For the present, one must be content with identifying the two conflicts that will shape our lives in all the years to come.

Index

Index